THE COMPREHENSIVE STUDY OF MUSIC
ANTHOLOGY OF MUSIC FROM DEBUSSY THROUGH STOCKHAUSEN

William Brandt
WASHINGTON STATE UNIVERSITY

Arthur Corra
ILLINOIS STATE UNIVERSITY

William Christ

Richard DeLone

Allen Winold
INDIANA UNIVERSITY

VOLUME IV

HARPER'S COLLEGE PRESS

A Department of Harper & Row, Publishers

NEW YORK   HAGERSTOWN   SAN FRANCISCO   LONDON

Text and Cover design by Jared Pratt
Music engraving by Armando Dal Molin, Music Typographers,
using the computerized system of Music Reprographics, Ltd.,
Oyster Bay, New York

THE COMPREHENSIVE STUDY OF MUSIC
Anthology of Music from Debussy through Stockhausen

Library of Congress Cataloging in Publication Data
Main entry under title:

The Comprehensive study of music.

CONTENTS: v. 1. Anthology of music from plainchant
through Gabrieli.—v. 2. Anthology of music from
Monteverdi to Mozart.—v. 3.
—v. 4. Anthology of music from Debussy to Stockhausen.
1. Instrumental music. 2. Vocal music. I. Brandt,
William E.
M2.C67   780   75-19402
ISBN 0-06-161420-3

FOREWORD TO THE SERIES

The history, literature, theory, and performance of music are all aspects of one indivisible whole, though as most introductory courses are taught today, there is little apparent sense of how intimately related they are. In general, a schism has developed in the training of musicians that has resulted in the compartmentalization of the materials of music into subjects taught (often out of sequence and independently) by different departments. Few attempts are made to wed these elements as they are indissolubly wed in the on-going stream of music history and performance.

However, since the pioneering efforts of the Juilliard School (in its "Literature and Materials" course) and of subsequent work done by the School of Music, Indiana University, and by other institutions taking part in the Ford Foundation Contemporary Music Project (CMP), forward-looking music educators have realized the importance of reuniting the theoretical materials of music with music history and literature, and with aspects of performance. The experimentation with the new methodology demonstrated conclusively (but not really surprisingly) that integrated study of the materials of music is virtually impossible without a set of instructional materials that are well-organized and that cover each area adequately. Ideally, courses designed for such comprehensive study should not only develop the knowledge of how music is constructed, but should also trace the evolution of musical styles, performance practices, and music history and literature in a logical, coherent sequence.

Challenged by the difficulty and importance of creating suitable materials for such a coordinated approach, we have developed *The Comprehensive Study of Music*—a series of anthologies of musical works, theory and history textbooks, and other instructional materials that provide an integrated program of study for undergraduate music majors.

The basic goals of *The Comprehensive Study of Music* are to assist the student of music in acquiring knowledge of:

1. Important musical works representing the historical and theoretical aspects of music
2. The sociocultural contexts from which the works emerged
3. The intrinsic characteristics of individual works and the basic principles they share with works of other styles, periods, and genres
4. Techniques of analysis, writing, and listening that evolve from the study of music literature
5. Significant composers and their works within the context of major developments in music
6. The techniques and skills needed for music reading, dictation, and keyboard harmony

The scope of the program is large, embracing most of the activities or disciplines traditionally associated with music study—analysis, writing, reading, performing, improvising, listening, and doing research on theoretical and historical subjects. Though we cover many genres, styles, and works, we believe it will be more helpful for the student to penetrate deeply into a limited number of works than to study many superficially. Another of the most important themes throughout *The Comprehensive Study of Music* is the relation between academic and applied music studies, and we make frequent suggestions regarding ways theoretical and historical matters may be related to performance practice.

Lastly, though the series is designed for use in courses in which at least some aspects of instruction in music theory and music literature are integrated, individual volumes may also be used in separate courses in each of these disciplines. The complete series contains the following:

ANTHOLOGIES OF MUSIC

Volume I   Plainchant Through Gabrieli (*forthcoming*)
Volume II   Monteverdi Through Mozart (*available now*)
Volume III Beethoven Through Wagner (*available now*)
Volume IV Debussy Through Stockhausen (*available now*)
Volume V   Piano Reductions for Harmonic Study (*forthcoming*)

CORE TEXTS FOR HISTORY AND THEORY

Volume VI   Basic Principles of Music Theory (*forthcoming*)
Volume VII Plainchant Through Gabrieli (*forthcoming*)
Volume VIII Monteverdi Through Mozart (*forthcoming*)
Volume IX   Beethoven Through Wagner (*forthcoming*)
Volume X   Debussy Through Stockhausen (*forthcoming*)

ADDITIONAL MATERIALS

Volume XI Melodic Ear Training and Sight Reading (*forthcoming*)
Volume XII Harmonic Ear Training and Keyboard Realization (*forthcoming*)

The Authors

ACKNOWLEDGMENTS

"The Monk and His Cat" from *Hermit Songs* by Samuel Barber. Copyright 1954
by G. Schirmer, Inc. Used by permission.

"Subject and Reflection" by Béla Bartók from *Mikrokosmos*, Volume 6.
Copyright 1940 by Hawkes & Son (London) Ltd; Renewed 1967.
Reprinted by permission of Boosey & Hawkes, Inc.

"Bulgarian Rhythm, Number 2" by Béla Bartók from *Mikrokosmos*, Volume 4.
Copyright 1940 by Hawkes & Son (London) Ltd; Renewed 1967.
Reprinted by permission of Boosey & Hawkes, Inc.

"Ostinato" by Béla Bartók from *Mikrokosmos*, Volume 6. Copyright 1940 by
Hawkes & Son (London) Ltd; Renewed 1967. Reprinted by permission of
Boosey & Hawkes, Inc.

String Quartet No. 2, Op. 17 by Béla Bartók. Copyright 1920; Renewed 1948.
Copyright and Renewal assigned to Boosey & Hawkes, Inc. for the U.S.A.
Reprinted by permission.

Music for Strings, Percussion, and Celeste, Movement II by Béla Bartók.
Copyright 1937 by Universal Edition; Renewed 1964. Copyright and
Renewal assigned to Boosey & Hawkes, Inc., for the U.S.A.
Reprinted by permission.

Tempi Concertati by Luciano Berio. Copyright © 1962 by Universal Edition S.p.A.
Milano. Used by permission.

Piano Sonata, Movement II by Elliot Carter. Copyright 1948, Mercury Music
Corporation. Used by permission.

Third Symphony by Aaron Copland. Copyright 1942 by Aaron Copland;
Renewed 1974. Reprinted by permission of Aaron Copland. Copyright
Owner, and Boosey & Hawkes, Inc., Sole Publishers and Licensees.

Mario Davidovsky's *Synchronisms No. 3*. Copyright © 1966 by Josef Marx,
McGinnis & Marx Music Publishers, 201 West 86th Street, #706,
New York, New York 10024; used by permission.

Little Chamber Music for Five Winds, Op. 24 by Paul Hindemith. Copyright 1922
by B. Schott's Soehne. Copyright renewed 1949. Used with permission.
All rights reserved.

The Unanswered Question by Charles E. Ives. Copyright 1908 by
Peer-Southern Organization. Reprinted by permission.

Canzone da Sonar by Thom Mason. Copyright © 1974 by Southern Music
Company, San Antonio, Texas 78292. Used by permission.

Wind Quintet, Op. 26 by Arnold Schoenberg. Copyright 1925 by Universal
Edition. Copyright renewed 1952 by Gertrude Schoenberg. Used by
permission of Belmont Music Publishers, Los Angeles, California 90049.

Klavierstück No. 8 by Karlheinz Stockhausen. Copyright 1954 by Universal
Edition A.G. Used by permission.

Suite from *L'Histoire du Soldat* by Igor Stravinsky. With permission of
J & W Chester/Edition Wilhelm Hansen London Limited.

CONTENTS

PIANO PRELUDES

VOL. 1, NO. 6, FOOTSTEPS IN THE SNOW

CLAUDE DEBUSSY

Retenu _ _ _ // a Tempo

Plus lent

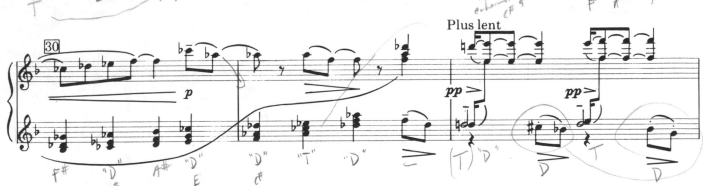

Très lent

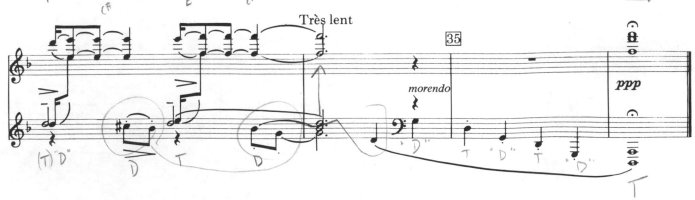

2 *Claude Debussy*

POUR LE PIANO

II. SARABANDE

CLAUDE DEBUSSY

Avec une élegance grave et lente

Animez un peu - - - - - - - -

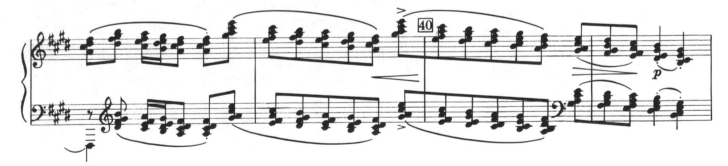

Au mouvement

8744

THREE NOCTURNES

I. NUAGES

CLAUDE DEBUSSY

sets up octatonic scale

based on
octatonic scale (G A♭ B♭ ...)

expressif

div. en 6

transitional

ROMANCE

CLAUDE DEBUSSY

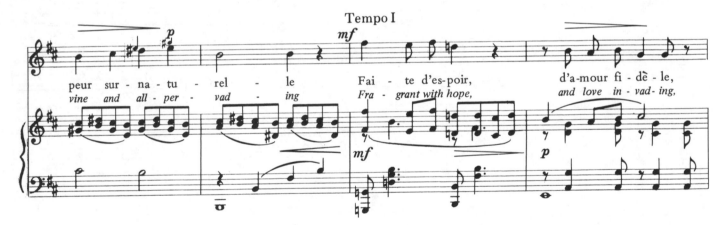

THE UNANSWERED QUESTION

CHARLES IVES

THREE PIANO PIECES, OP. 11, NO. 2

ARNOLD SCHOENBERG

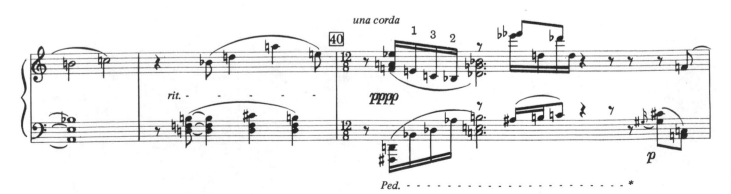

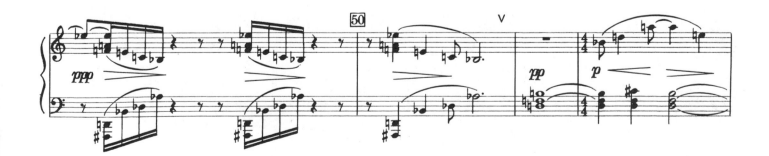

WIND QUINTET, OP. 26, NO. 3

ARNOLD SCHOENBERG

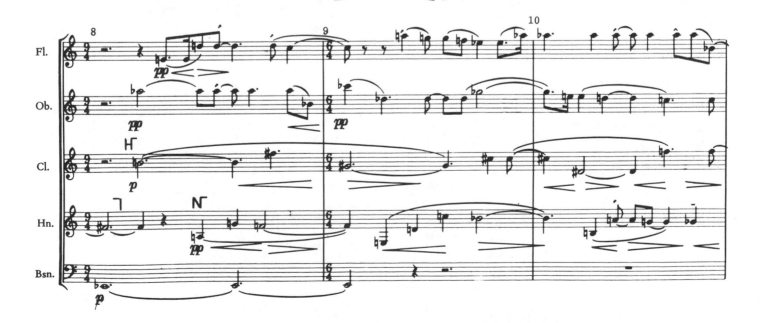

36   Arnold Schoenberg

PAVANE POUR UNE INFANTE DEFUNTE

FIRST SECTION

MAURICE RAVEL

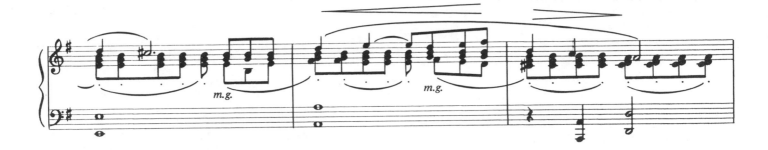

MOTHER GOOSE SUITE

I.   PAVANE DE LA BELLE AU BOIS DORMANT

MAURICE RAVEL

For two pianos

50   *Maurice Ravel*

MUSIC FOR STRINGS, PERCUSSION, AND CELESTE

SECOND MOVEMENT

BELA BARTOK

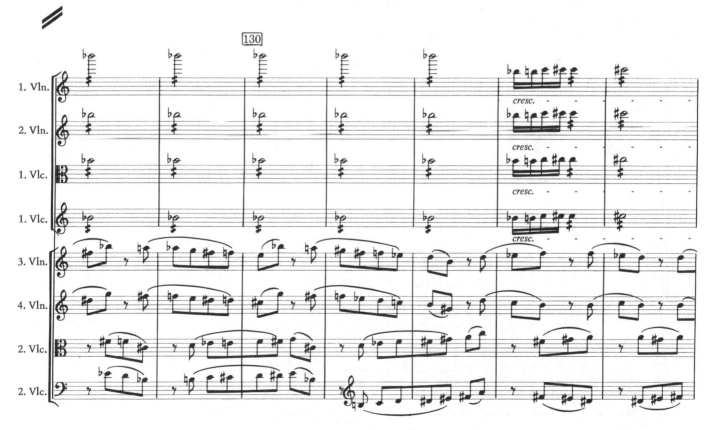

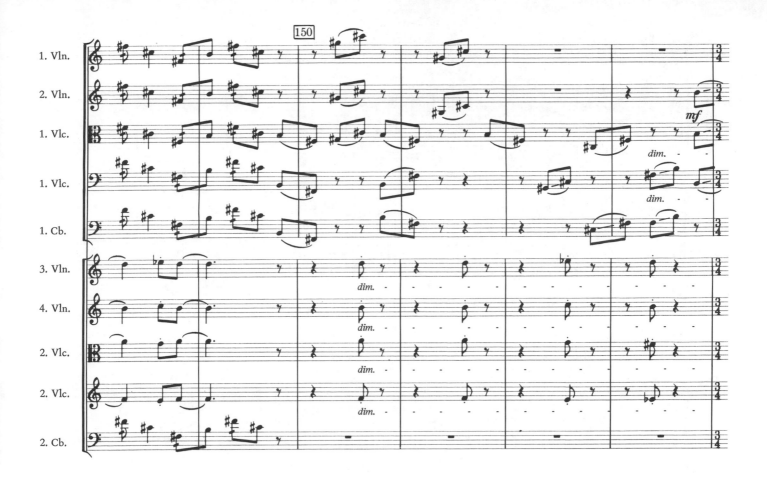

MUSIC FOR STRINGS, PERCUSSION, AND CELESTE **73**

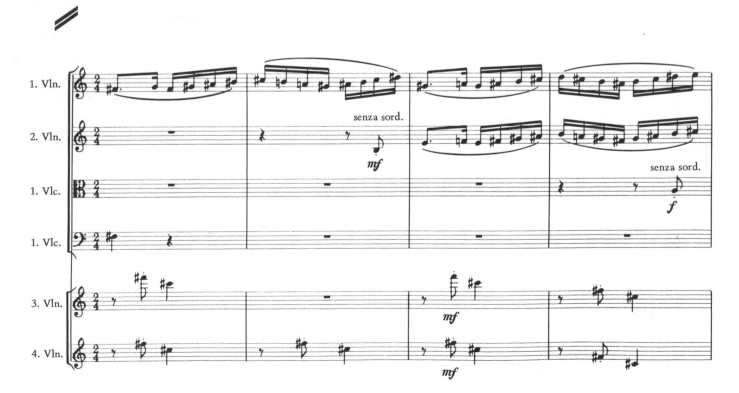

MIKROKOSMOS, VOL. 4

BULGARIAN RHYTHM, NO. 2

BELA BARTOK

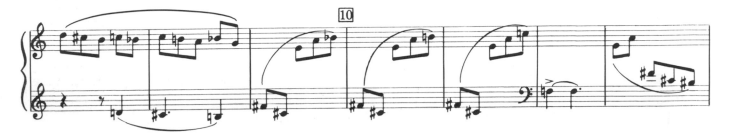

[23 sec.]

MIKROKOSMOS, VOL. 6

SUBJECT AND REFLECTION, EXCERPT

BELA BARTOK

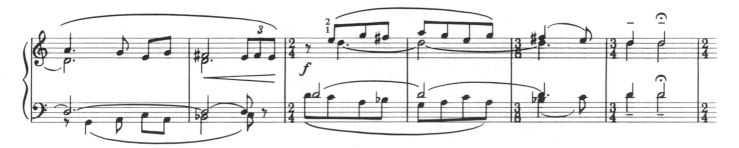

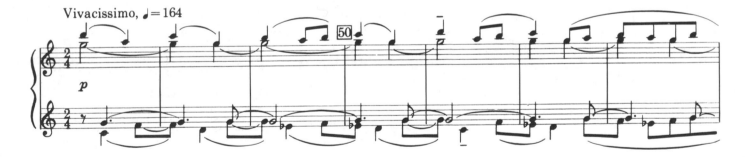

MIKROKOSMOS, VOL. 6

OSTINATO

BELA BARTOK

Vivacissimo, ♩=176-168

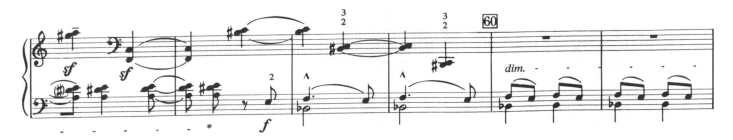

[2 min. 5 sec.]

SECOND STRING QUARTET, OP. 17, NO. 3

BELA BARTOK

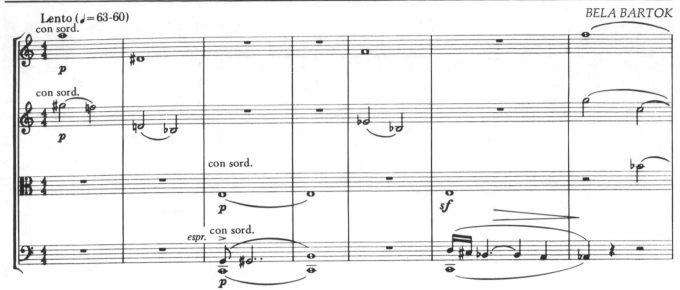

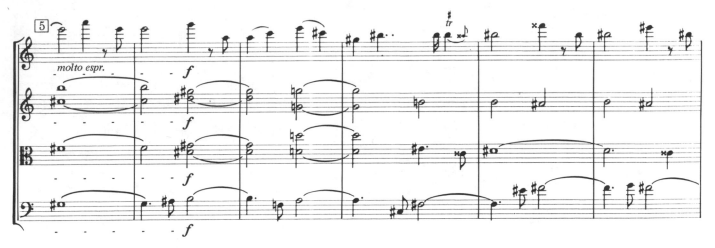

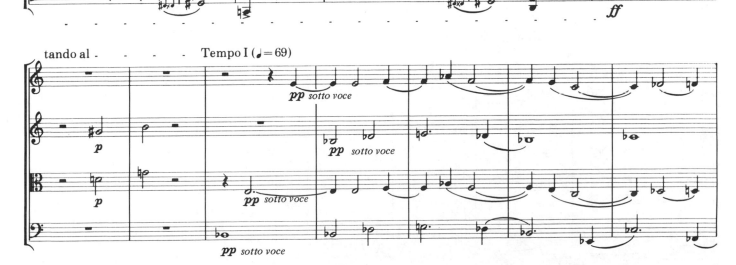

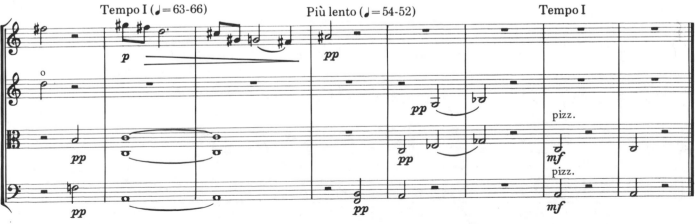

SUITE DE L'HISTOIRE DU SOLDAT
POUR CLARINETTE, VIOLON, ET PIANO

I. MARCHE DU SOLDAT

IGOR STRAVINSKY

100   Igor Stravinsky

III. PETIT CONCERT

excessivement court

PETIT CONCERT   103

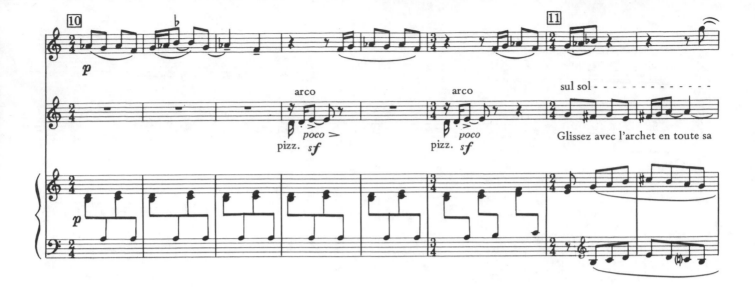

108   *Igor Stravinsky*

V. DANSE DU DIABLE

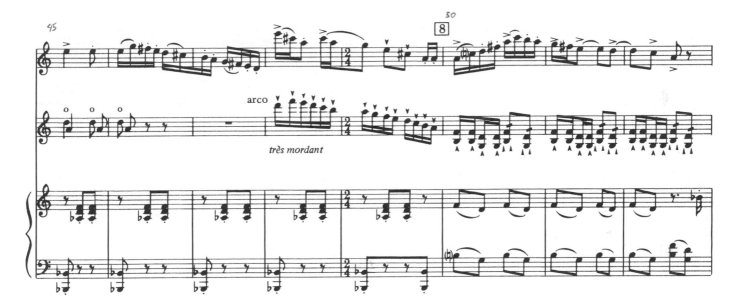

LES NOCES

PART ONE

IGOR STRAVINSKY

On tres - se, on tres-se-ra la tres-se `a Nas-ta-sie, on tres-se-ra la tresse `a

Ti - mo-fè-ev - na, la tresse on pei-gne-ra puis la tres - se on tres-se -

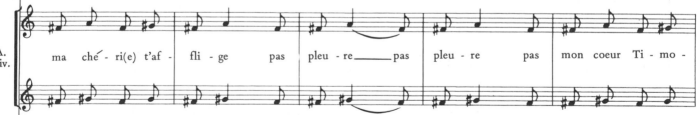

120   *Igor Stravinsky*

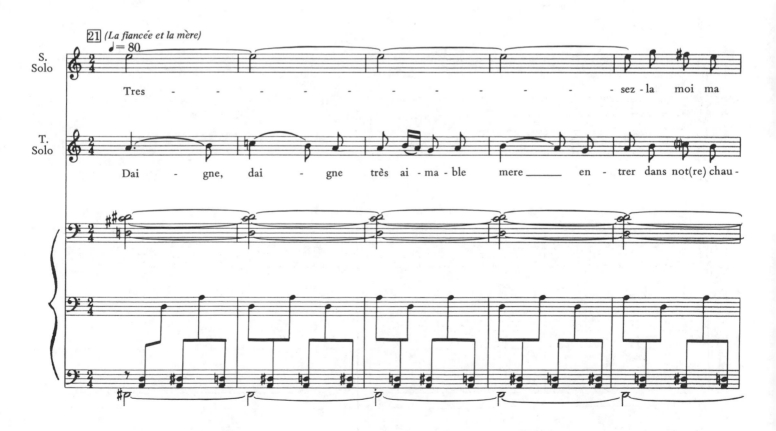

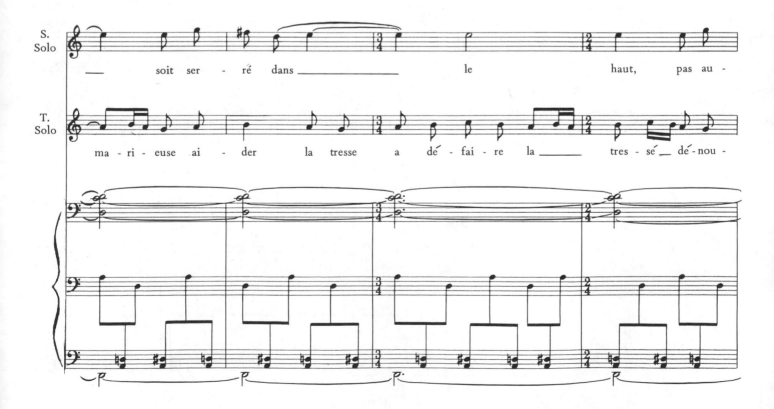

CANTICUM SACRUM AD HONOREM SANCTI MARCI NOMINIS

DEDICATIO

IGOR STRAVINSKY

I. EUNTES IN MUNDUM

II. SURGE, AQUILO

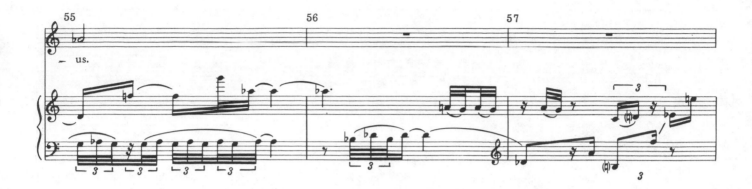

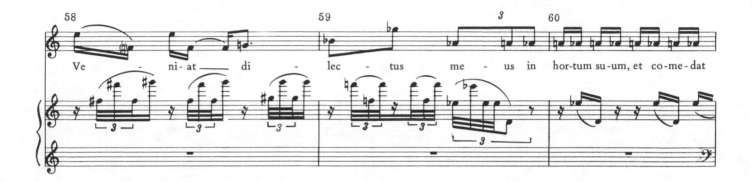

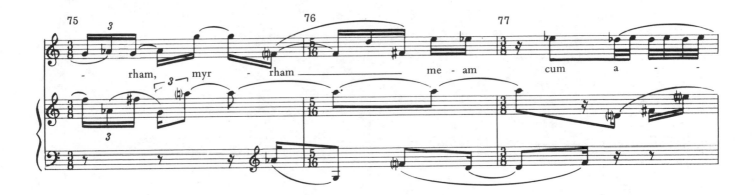

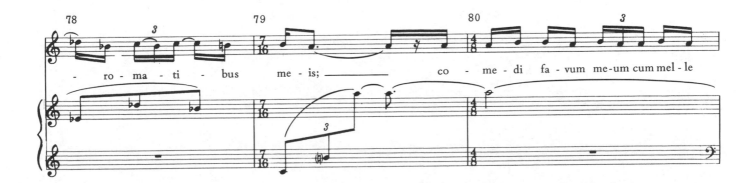

CONCERT FOR FLUTE, OBOE, CLARINET, HORN, TRUMPET, TROMBONE, VIOLIN, VIOLA, AND PIANO, OP. 24

FIRST MOVEMENT

ANTON WEBERN

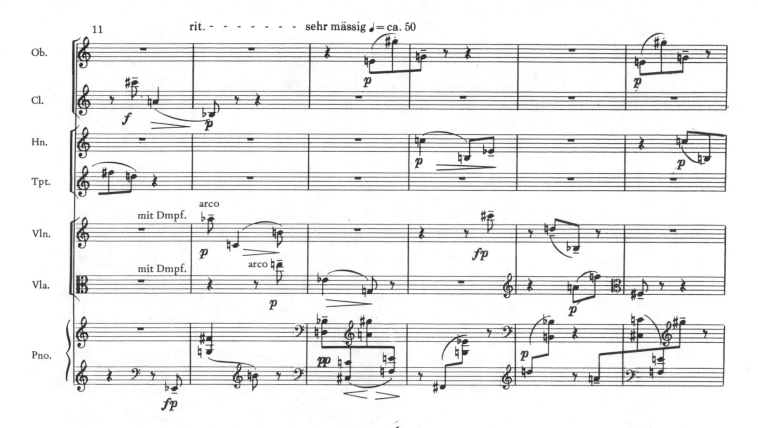

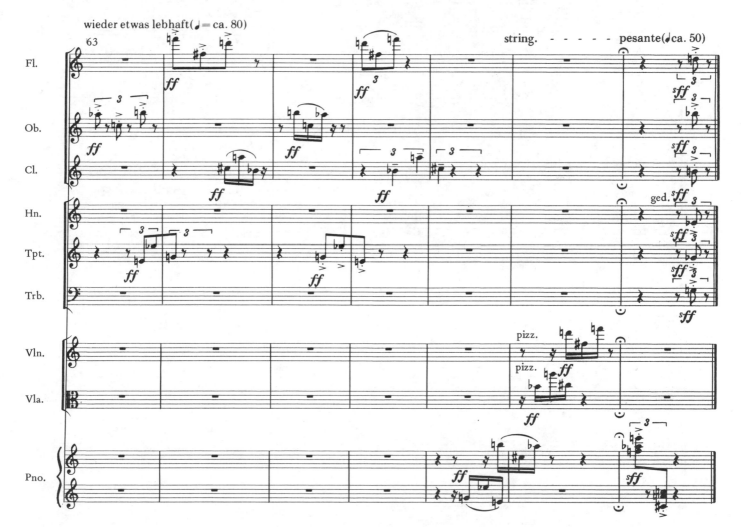

SIX SONGS, OP. 14

ANTON WEBERN

Vocal text (line 1): schwar - zem Kahn hin - ü - ber - star - ben Lie - ben - de.

Vocal text (line 2): O - der es läu - ten die Schritte E - lis' durch den Hain den hy - a -

Vocal text (line 3): zin - the - nen wie - der ver - hal - lend un - ter Ei - chen. O des

Fliessend (♪ = ca 120)

DENSITY 21.5

EDGAR VARESE

For solo flute

♩ = 72 **

(sharply articulated)***

* Written in January, 1936, at the request of Georges Barrere for the inauguration of his platinum flute. Revised April, 1946. 21.5 is the density of platinum.

** Always strictly in time — follow metronomic indications.

*** Notes marked + to be played softly, hitting the keys at the same time to produce a percussive effect.

LITTLE CHAMBER MUSIC FOR FIVE WINDS, OP. 24, NO. 2

FIRST MOVEMENT

PAUL HINDEMITH

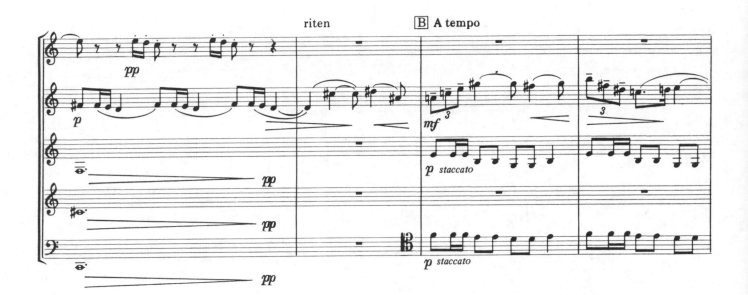

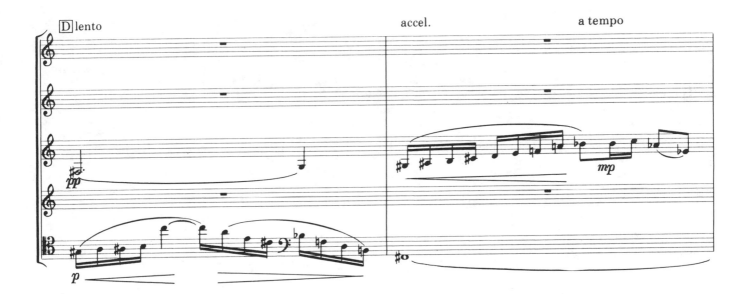

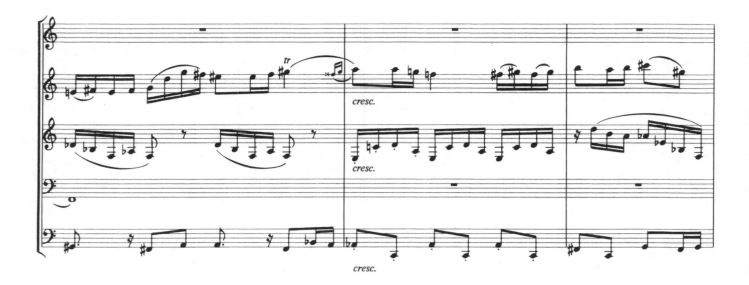

F Langsam

Wieder lustig

THIRD MOVEMENT

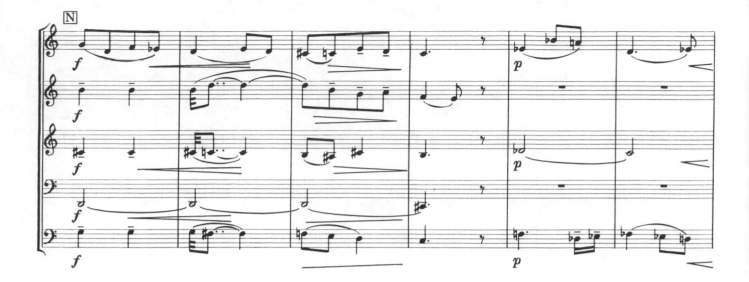

ritenuto

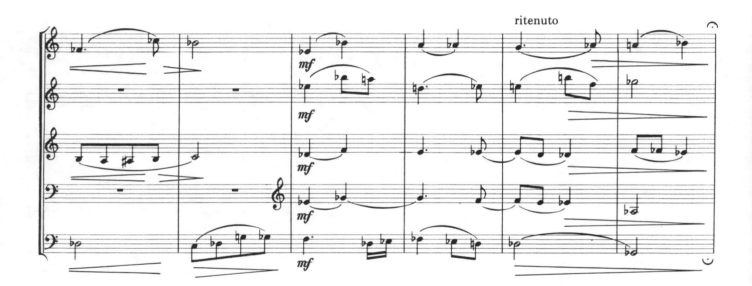

Im gleichen ruhigen Zeitmass (nicht scherzando!)

164   *Paul Hindemith*

THIRD SYMPHONY

SECOND MOVEMENT, FIRST SECTION

AARON COPLAND

194   Aaron Copland

PIANO SONATA

SECOND MOVEMENT

ELLIOT CARTER

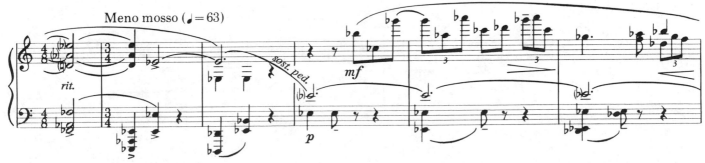

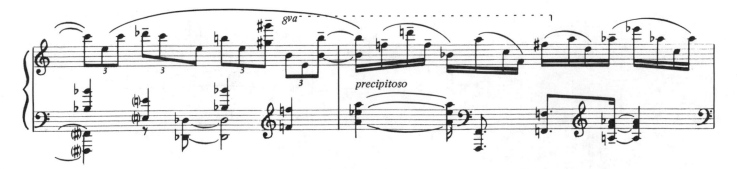

Più mosso (♩=80)

animando poco a poco

[animando]

meno mosso

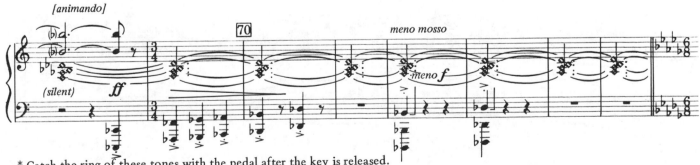

* Catch the ring of these tones with the pedal after the key is released.

Misterioso (♩. = ca. 132)
(Tempo rubato)

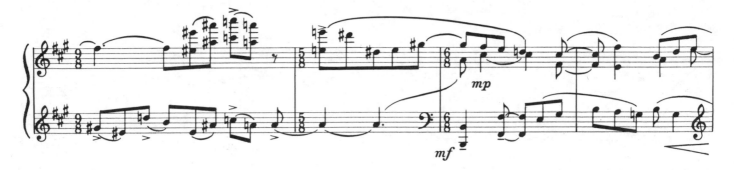

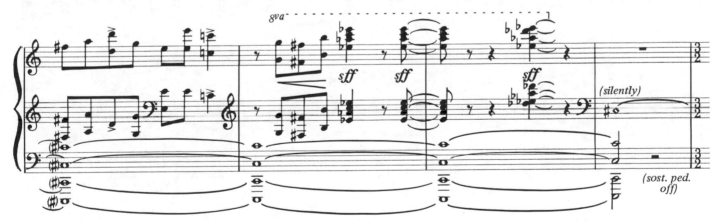

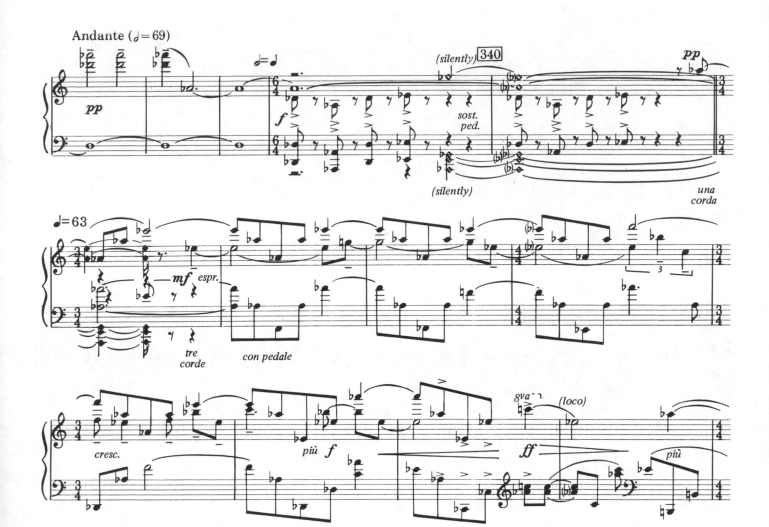

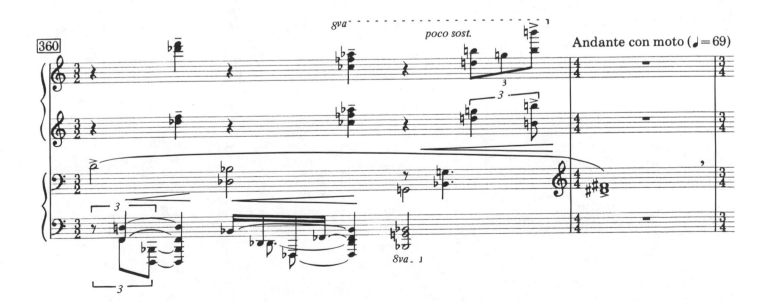

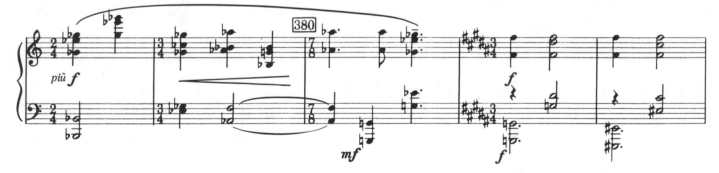

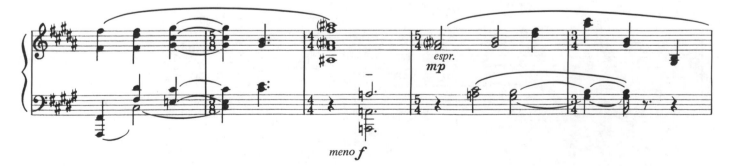

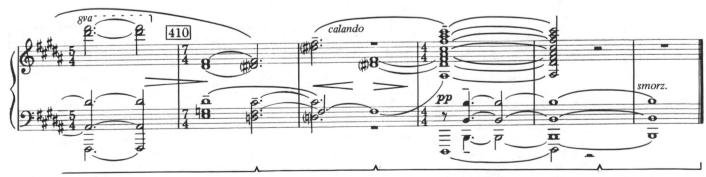

raise pedal slowly

SAMUEL BARBER

8th or 9th century; translation by W.H. Auden used by special permission.

* Notes marked (−) in these two measures should be slightly longer, pochissimo rubato; also on the fourth page.

TEMPI CONCERTATI

(EXCERPTS FROM ORIGINAL SCORE, PAGES 22–44)

I

The four groups must be spaced as far as possible from each other. Especially the groups which are most similar to each other must be placed as far apart as possible: that is, group I far from IV and group II far from III. The most suitable arrangement will always be that which places the four groups around the audience. The flautist must be placed in a central position and must be visible to all the performers.

II

In a public performance the work should always be performed without a conductor, even though a conductor is always necessary for the preparation and rehearsals of the work. The gestures s t r i c t l y n e c e s s a r y to coordinate the performance will be made by the flautist and sometimes by the violinist and either of the two pianists.

In case the performing conditions absolutely require the presence of a conductor, he must never conduct the measures 71 to 110 and the measures 320 to 365. As often as possible he must give the task of synchronizing the performance to the flautist and the other instrumentalists who, from time to time, assume the role of guides and provide "signals" for the ensemble.

Certain conducting gestures (to be made, when possible, by the flautist) are of course indispensable.

The sign ➜ can correspond to a downward gesture,

the sign ↑ can correspond to a gesture to the right,

the sign ↙ can correspond to an upward gesture,

that is, similar to the gestures used to indicate a measure of three beats (without keeping a strict tempo however). It is preferable that the flautist gives these signs which have the evident scope of cueing the specified instruments, thus keeping the performance within the time limits suggested by the proportional distribution of the notes (cf paragraph III).

The small notes must always be performed as fast as possible. Only at page 62 and page 63 will they be performed according to the density pattern suggested (that is, an accelerando), in the order preferred by the performer and in the quantity the closest possible to the indicated one.

The sign ⌇ indicates a tremolo or trill which must be very rapid but discontinuous: in any case not periodic.

III

Beginning from measure 161, the ordinary rhythmic notation is gradually superseded by a proportional one where the absolute rhythmic values are not indicated but rather the relative time proportions. By their spacial distribution, the visual relations thus suggest time values which are conditioned by the preceding (or simultaneous) ordinary rhythmic notation and metronome values. The proportional notation should thus be intended as a development of the ordinary rhythmic notation, not a simplification of it.

LUCIANO BERIO

The notes ♪ must be performed "sciolte": their actual duration is determined by the manner of attack. The ♩ notes must last until the succeeding notes or silences, in proportion to the length of the crossbar ⌐

Unless otherwise indicated (such as by the sign ➡ at the beginning of a measure), an e x a c t synchronization of the parts written in proportional notation is not required or intended. The degree of approximation of the synchronization must however be prepared and predisposed during the rehearsals in accordance with the technical capabilities of each performer. The vertical dotted lines constitute above all a visual point of reference and thus suggest the average degree of approximation. Less synchronization is permitted when the sign ⌇ appears, and less still at the sign ⌇⌇

Elenco e raggruppamento degli strumenti

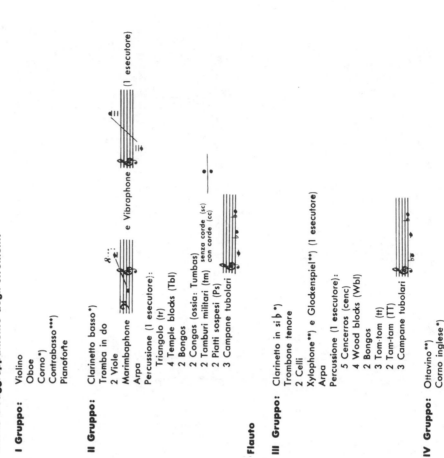

I Gruppo: Violino
Oboe
Corno*)
Contrabasso***)
Pianoforte

II Gruppo: Clarinetto basso*)
Tromba in do
2 Viole
Marimbaphone e Vibraphone (1 esecutore)
Arpa
Percussione (1 esecutore):
  Triangolo (tr)
  4 Temple blocks (Tbl)
  2 Bongos
  2 Congas (ossia: Tumbas)
  2 Tamburi militari (tm) senza corde (sc)
  2 Piatti sospesi (Ps) con corde (cc)
  3 Campane tubolari

Flauto

III Gruppo: Clarinetto in si♭*)
Trombone tenore
2 Celli
Xylophone**) e Glockenspiel**) (1 esecutore)
Arpa
Percussione (1 esecutore):
  5 Cencerros (cenc)
  4 Wood blocks (Wbl)
  2 Bongos
  3 Tom-tom (tt)
  2 Tam-tam (TT)
  3 Campane tubolari

IV Gruppo: Ottavino**)
Corno inglese*)
Clarinetto in si♭*)
Fagotto
Pianoforte e Celesta**) (1 esecutore)

*) Scritti in suoni reali   **) Scritti un'ottava sotto   ***) Scritto un'ottava sopra

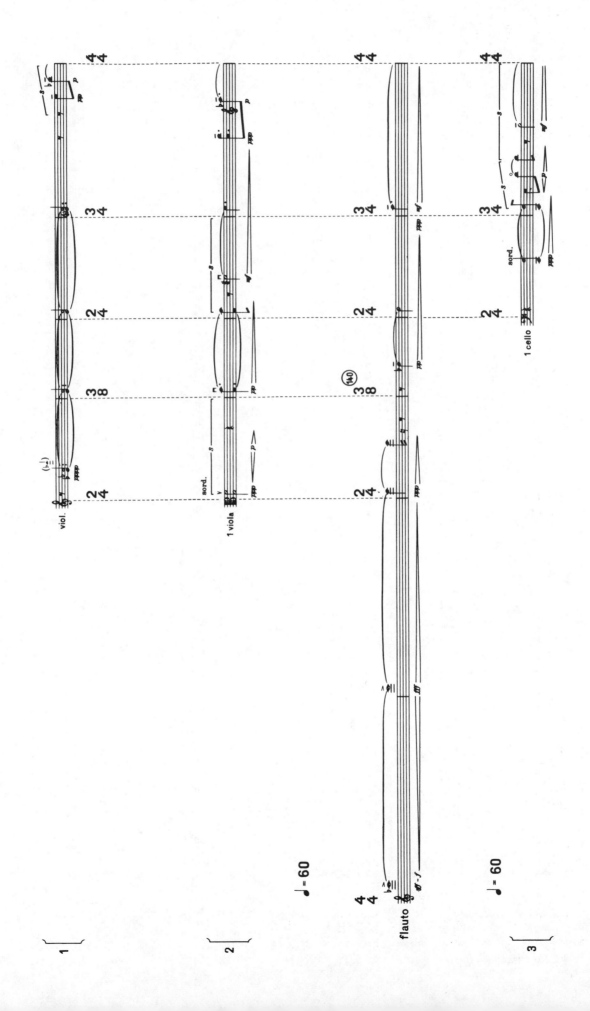

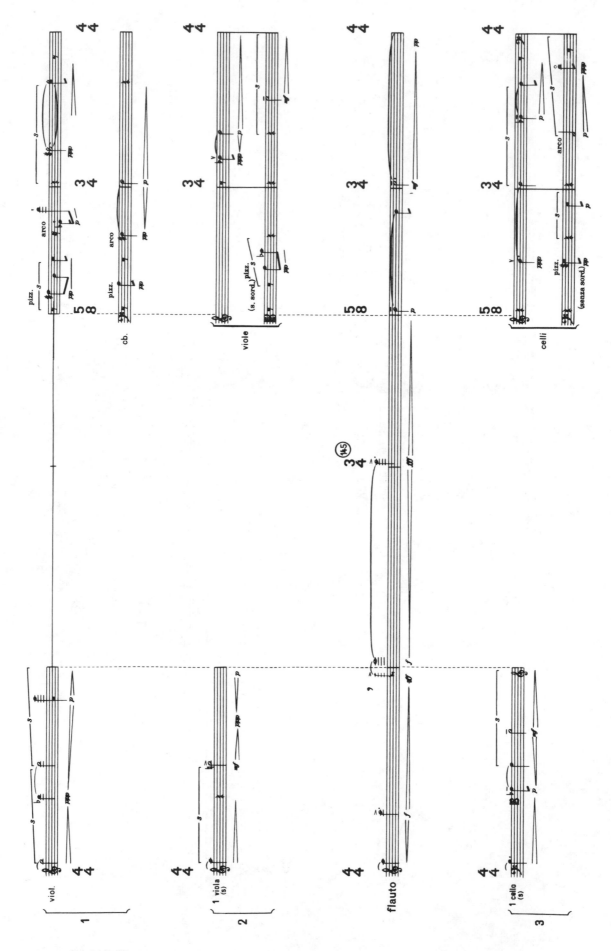

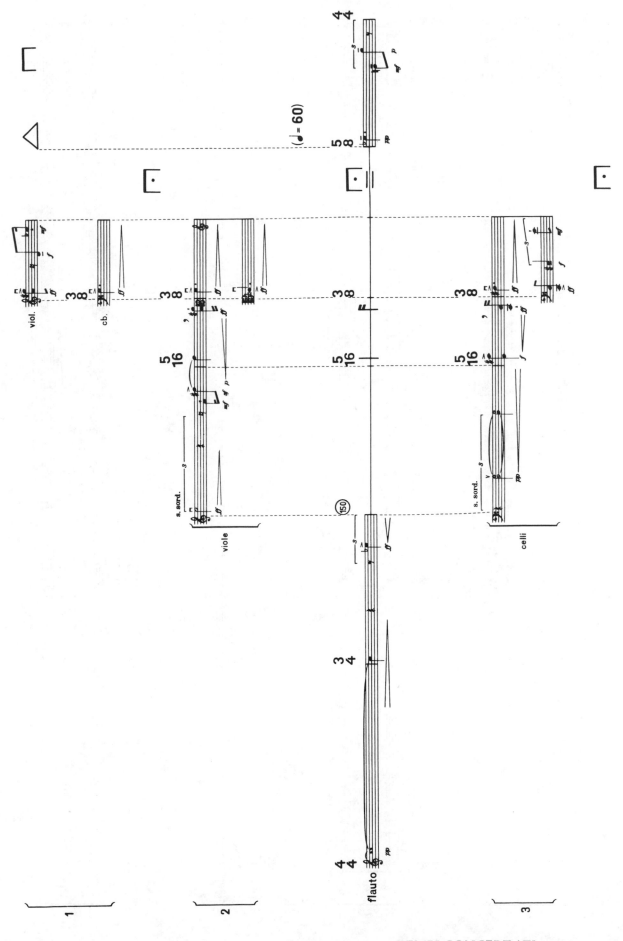

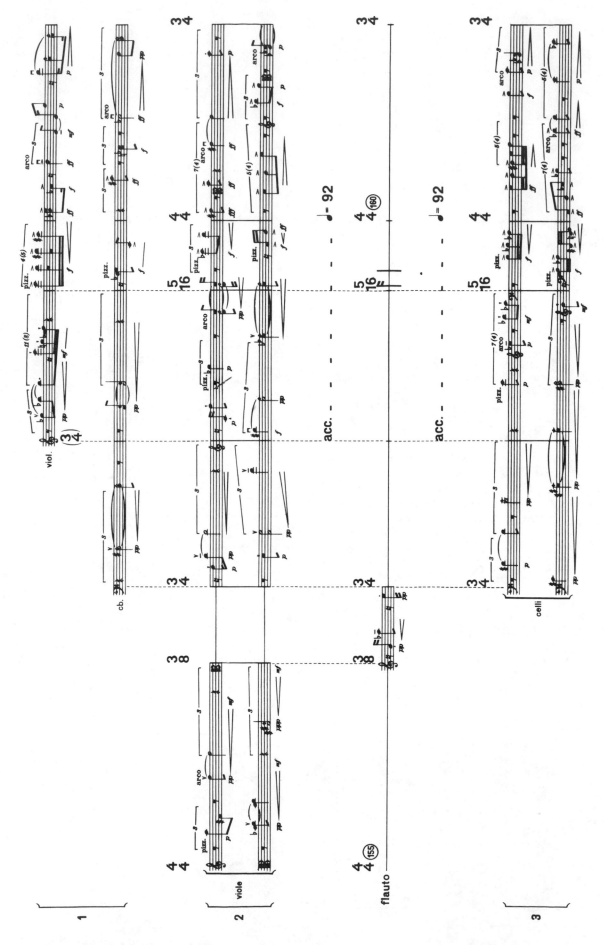

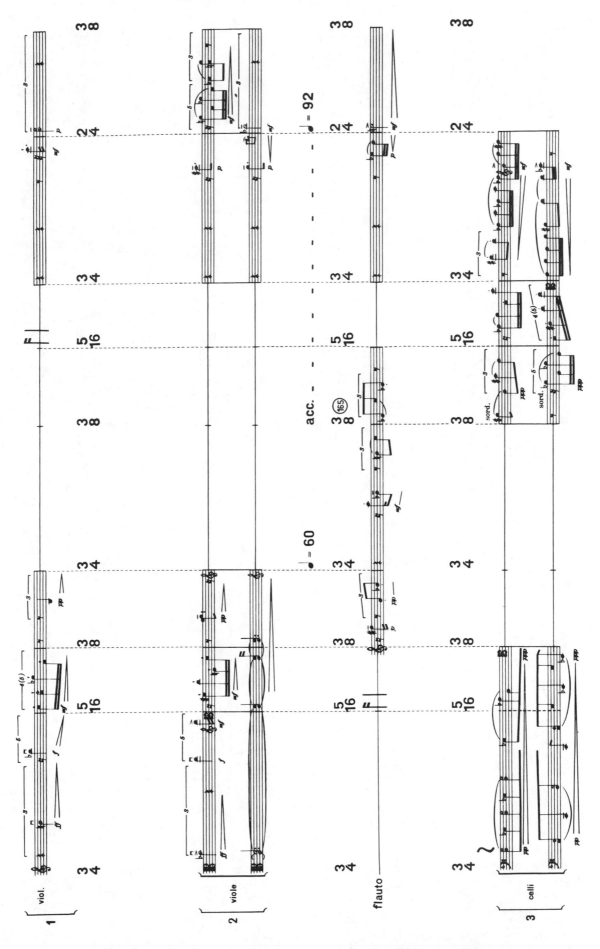

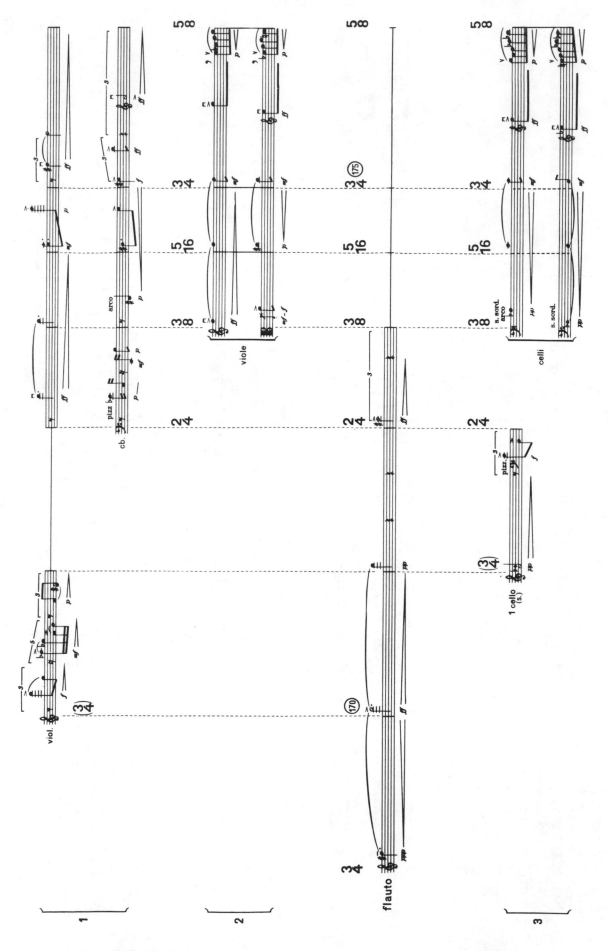

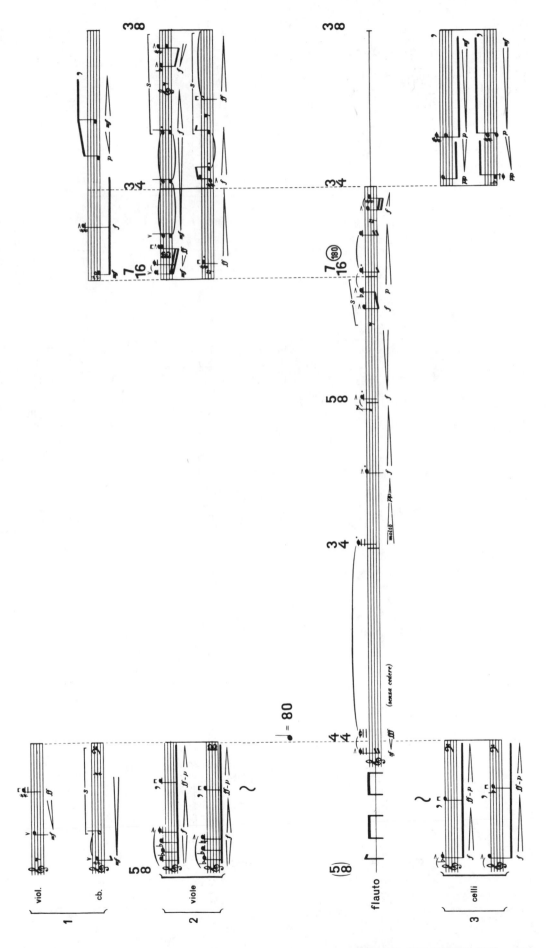

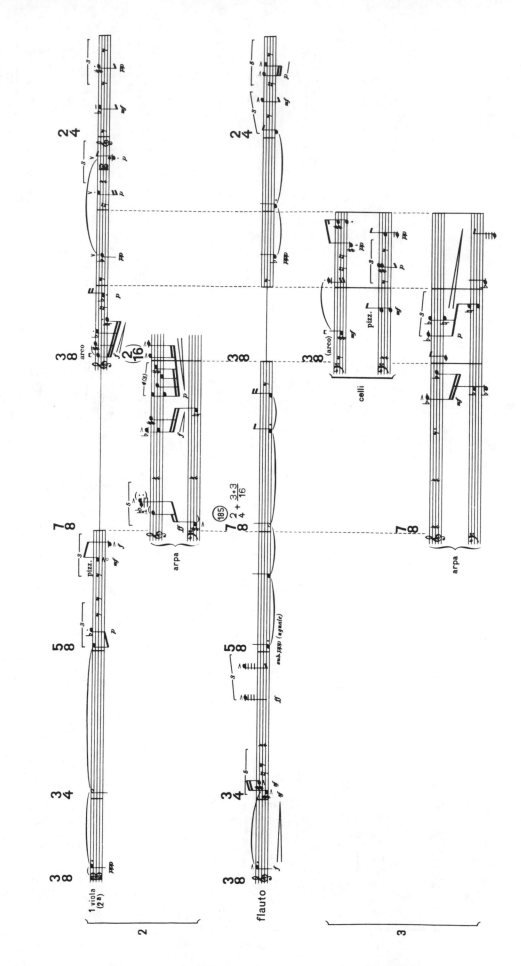

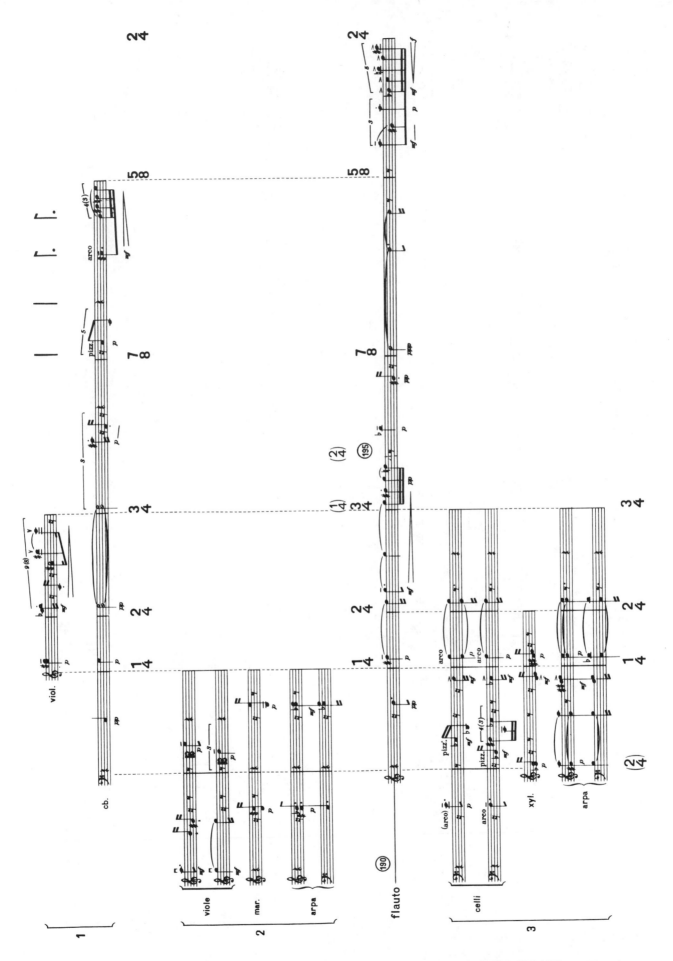

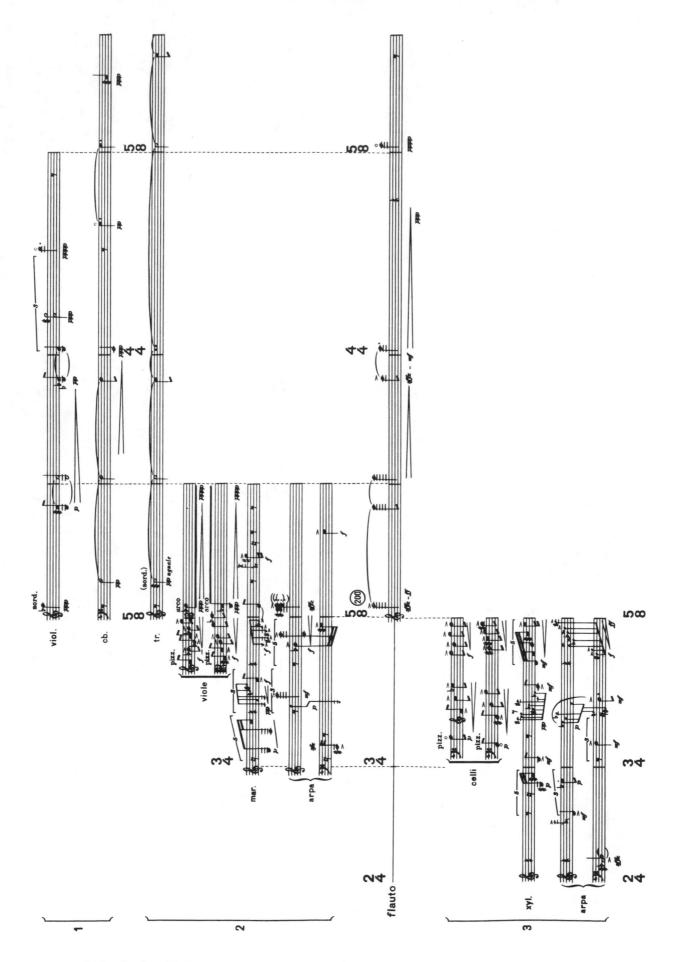

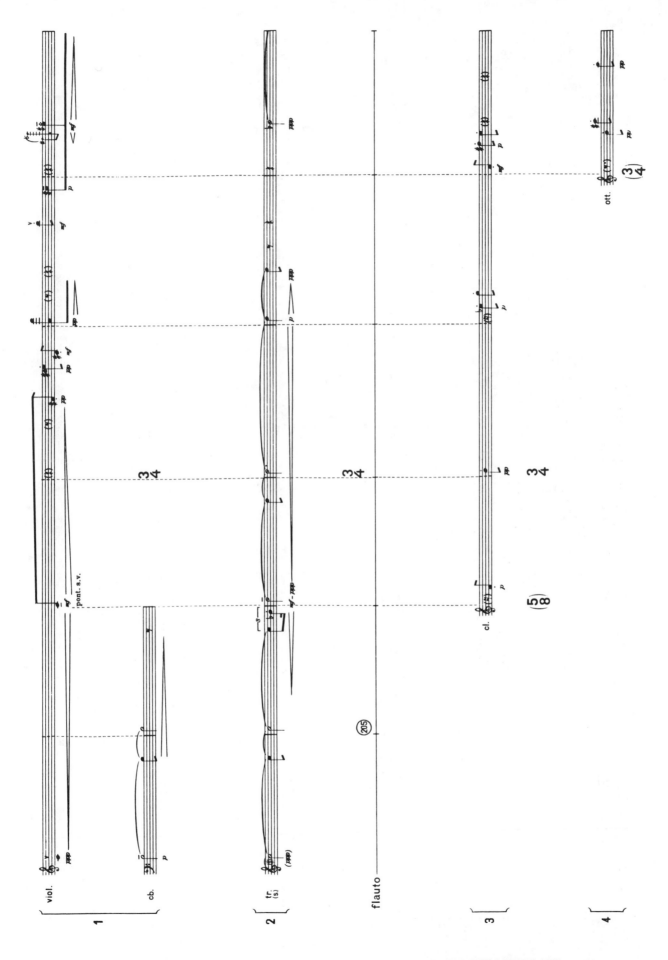

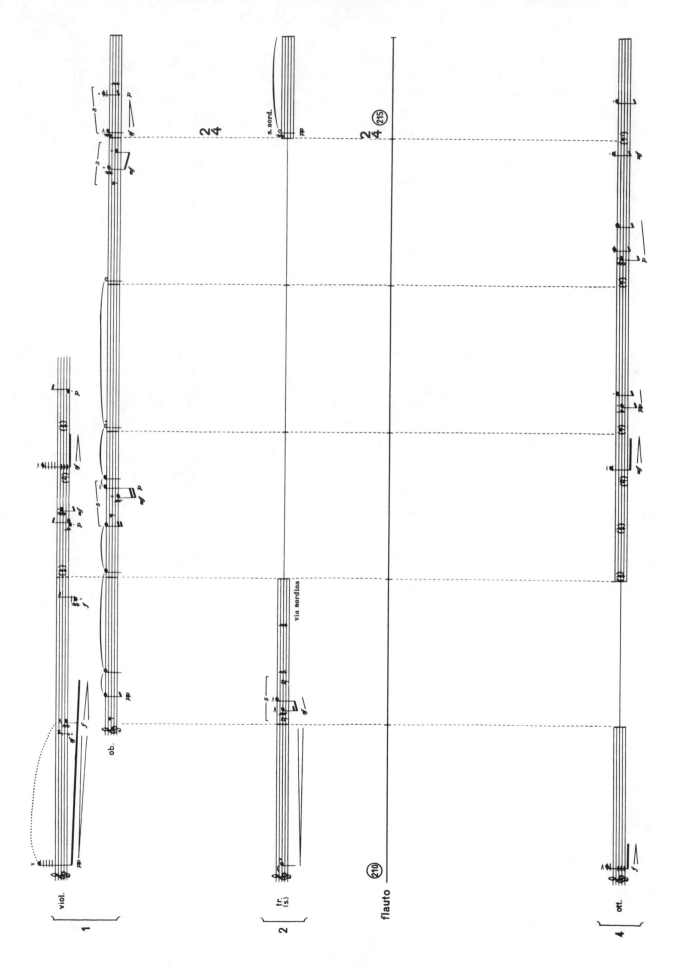

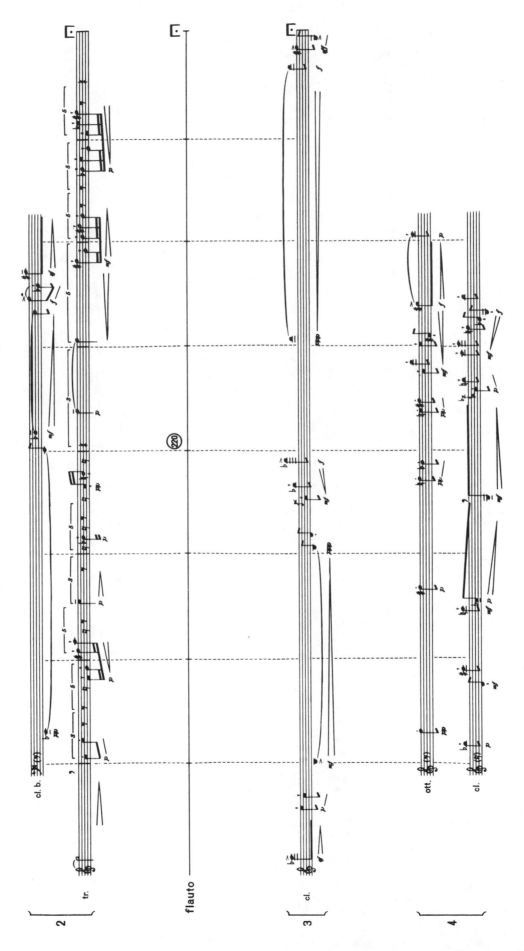

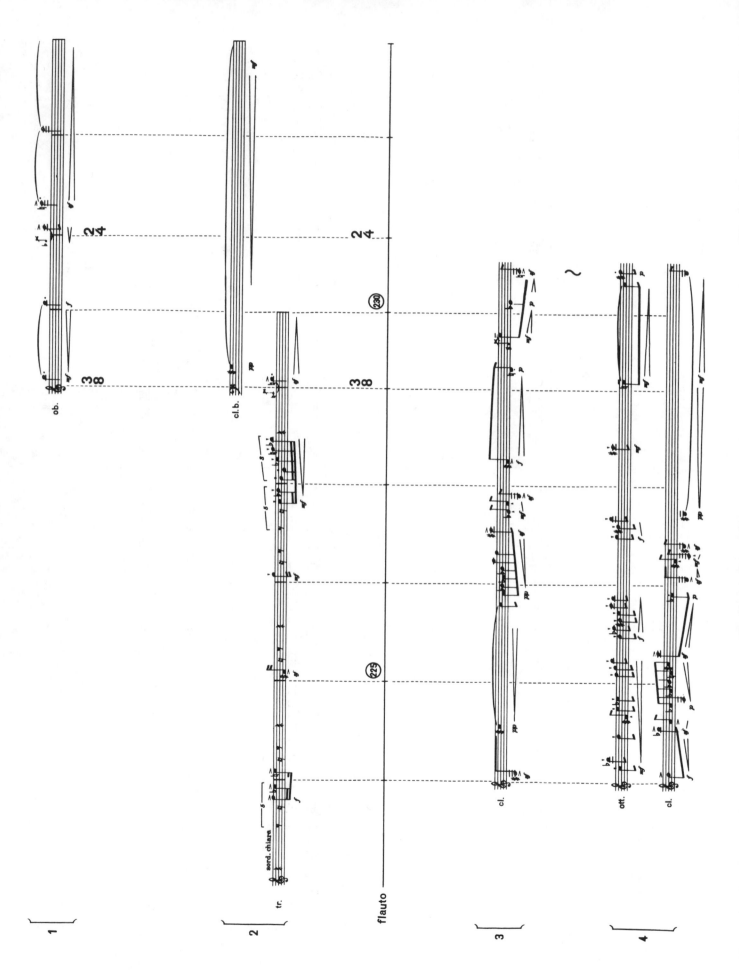

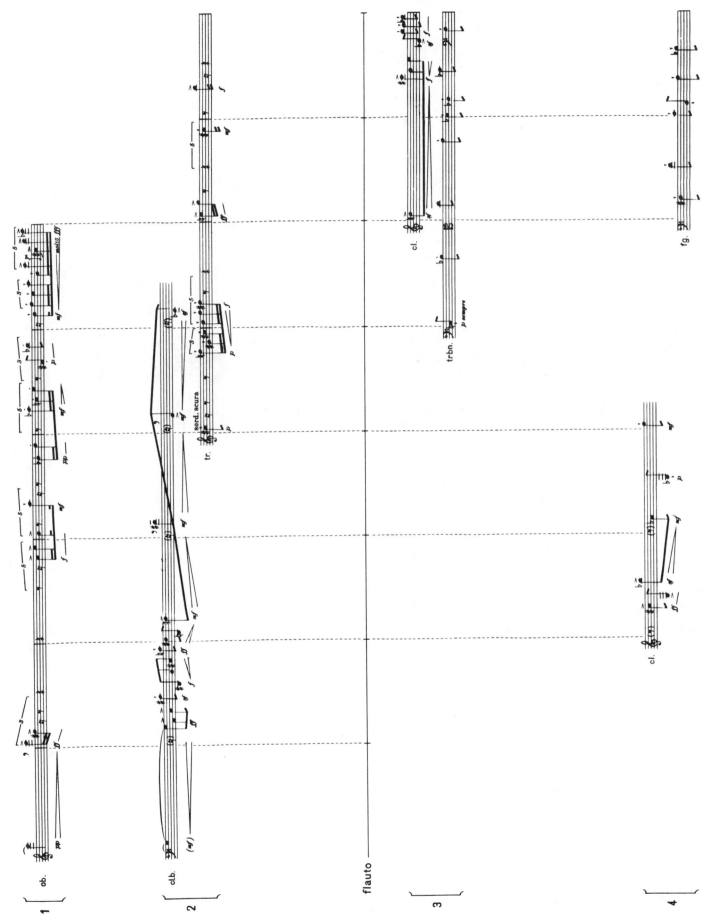

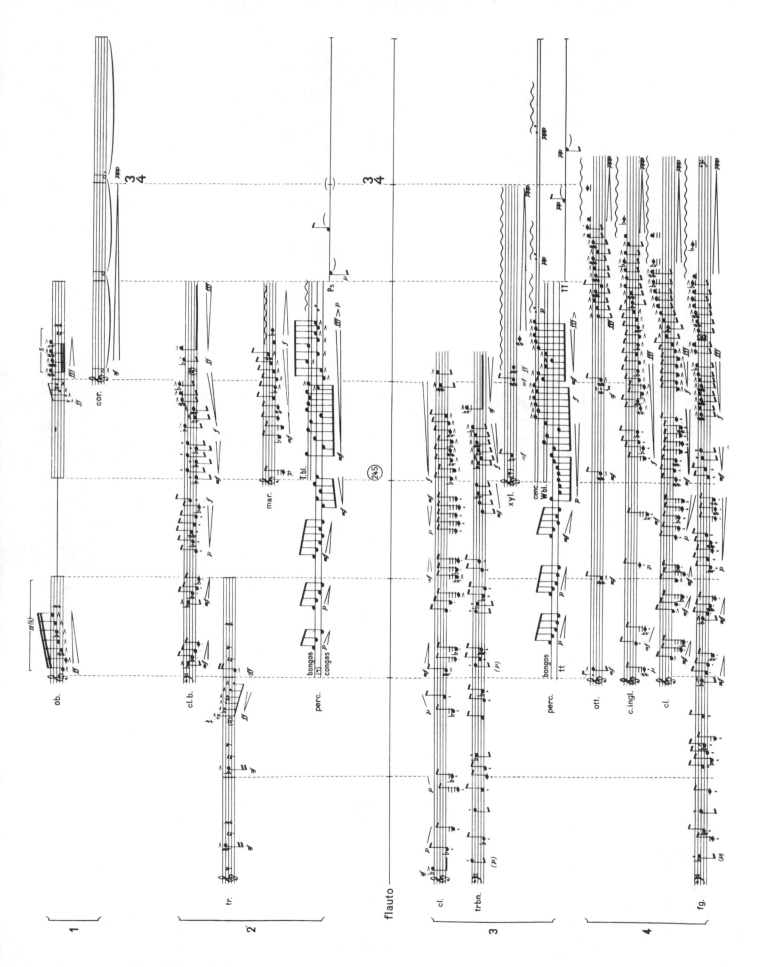

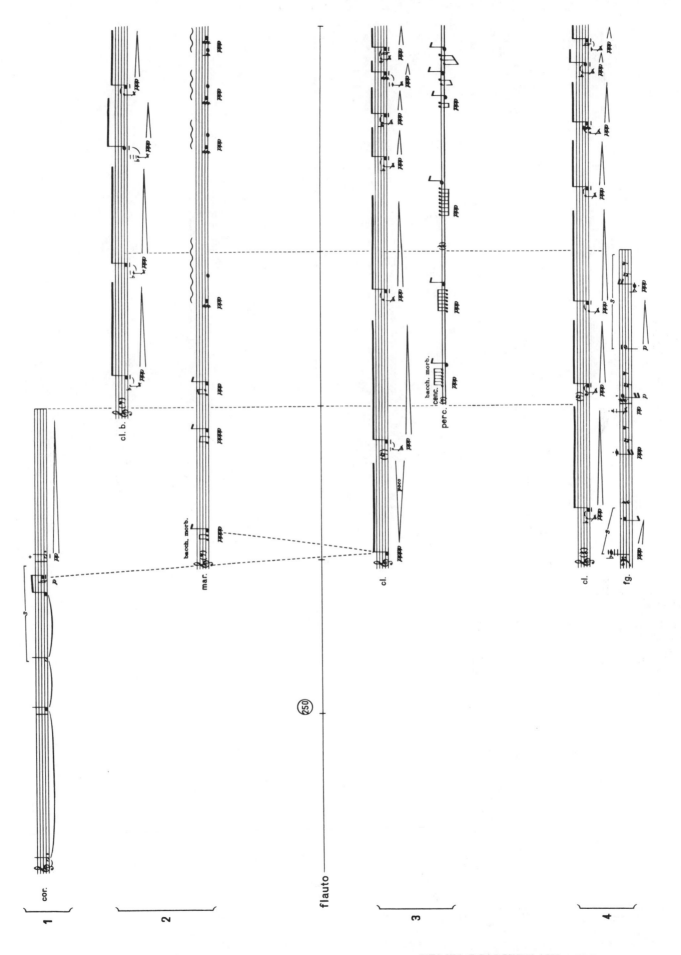

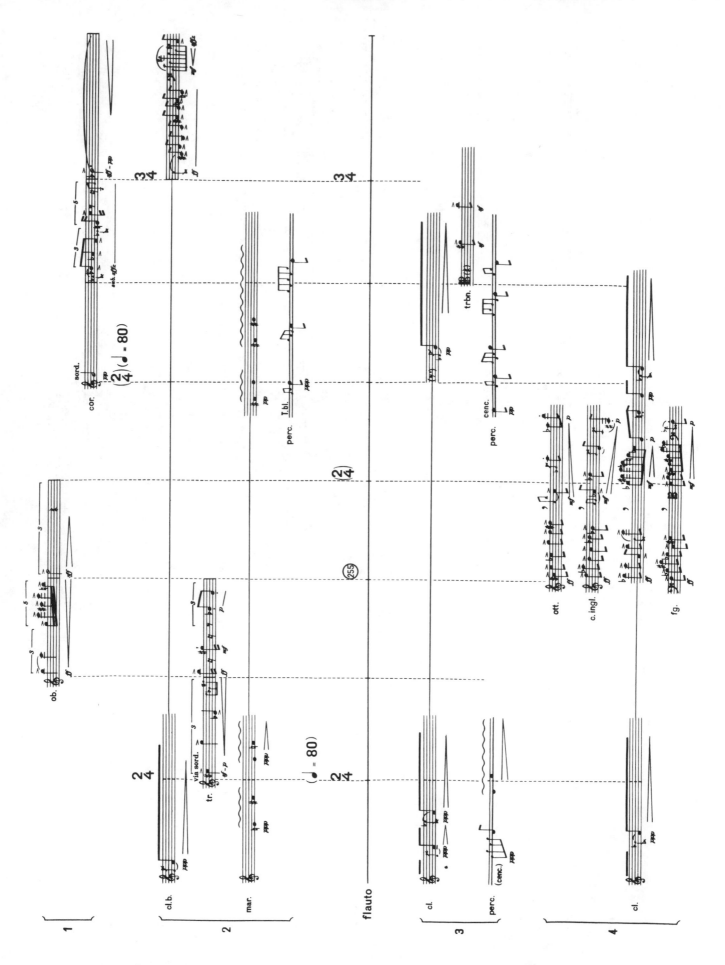

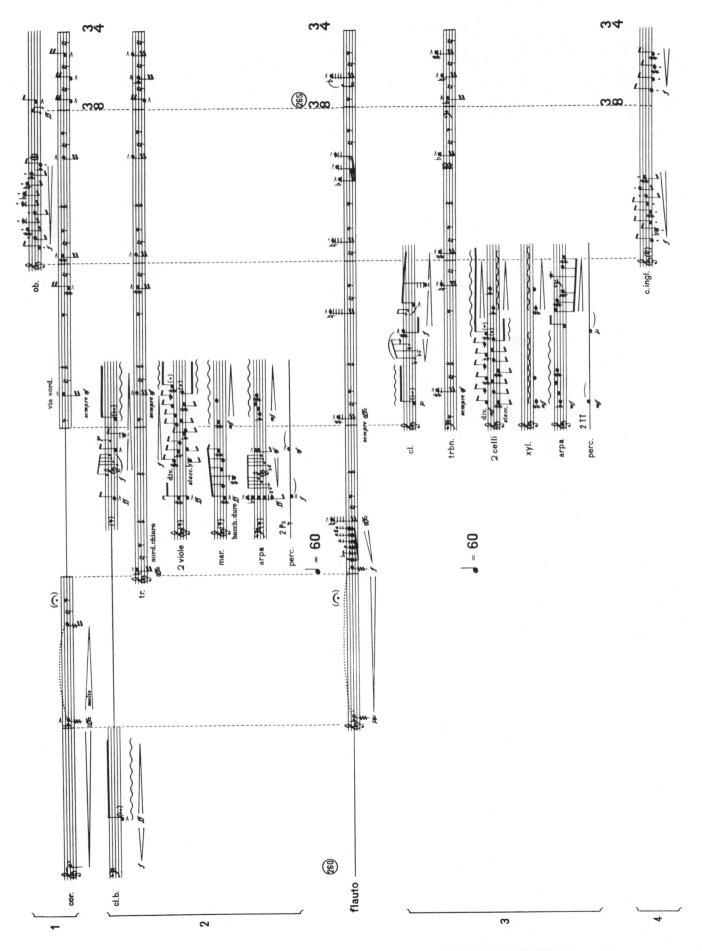

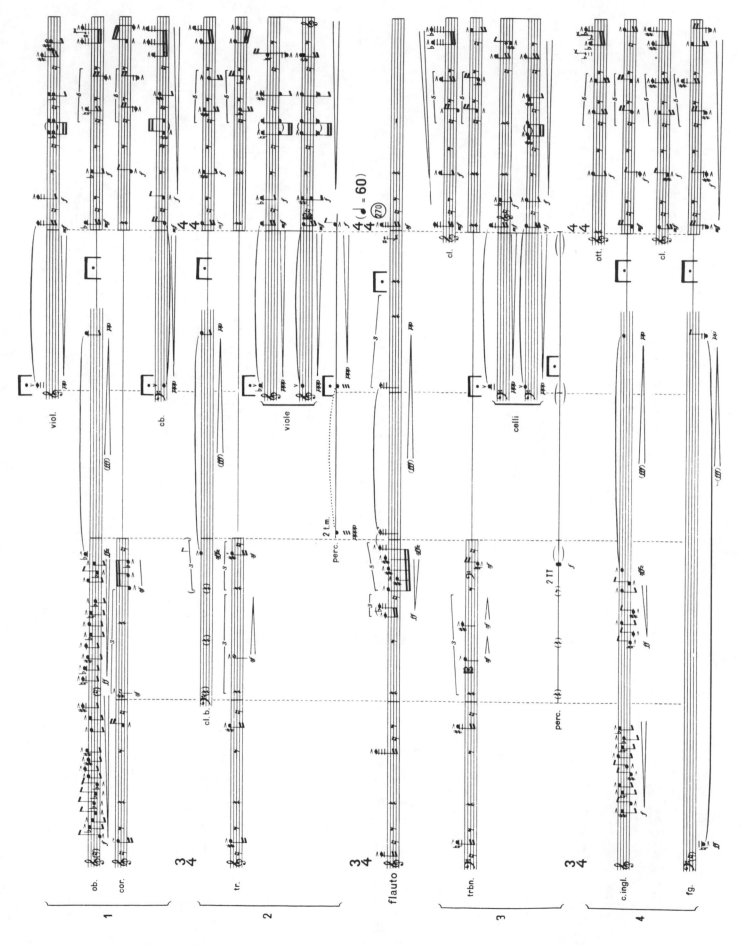

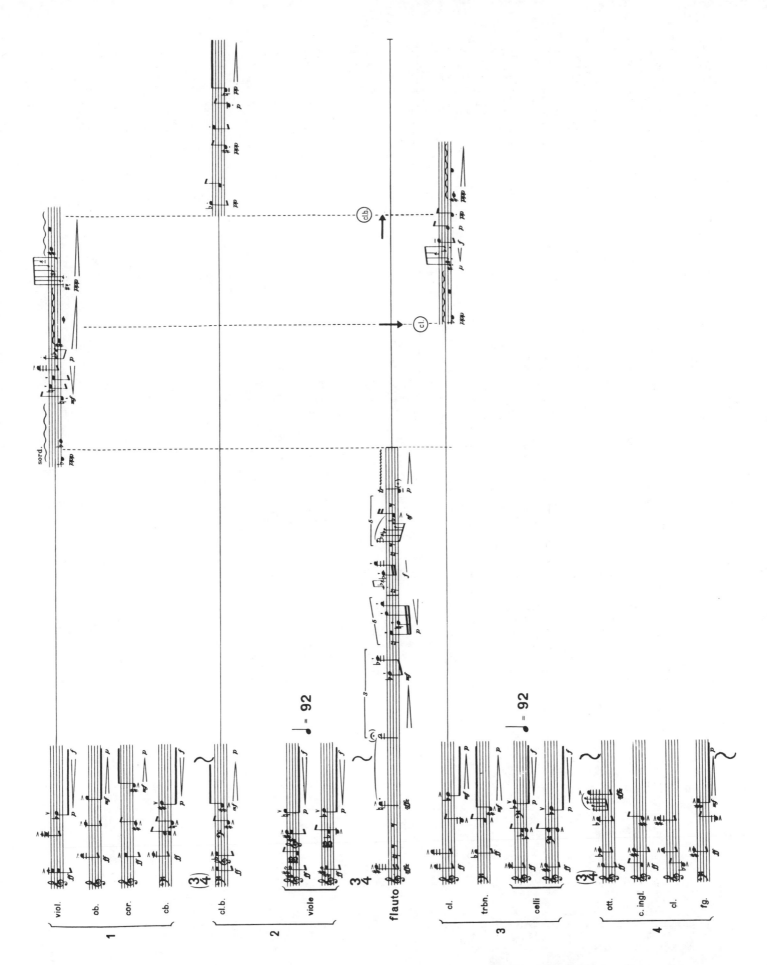

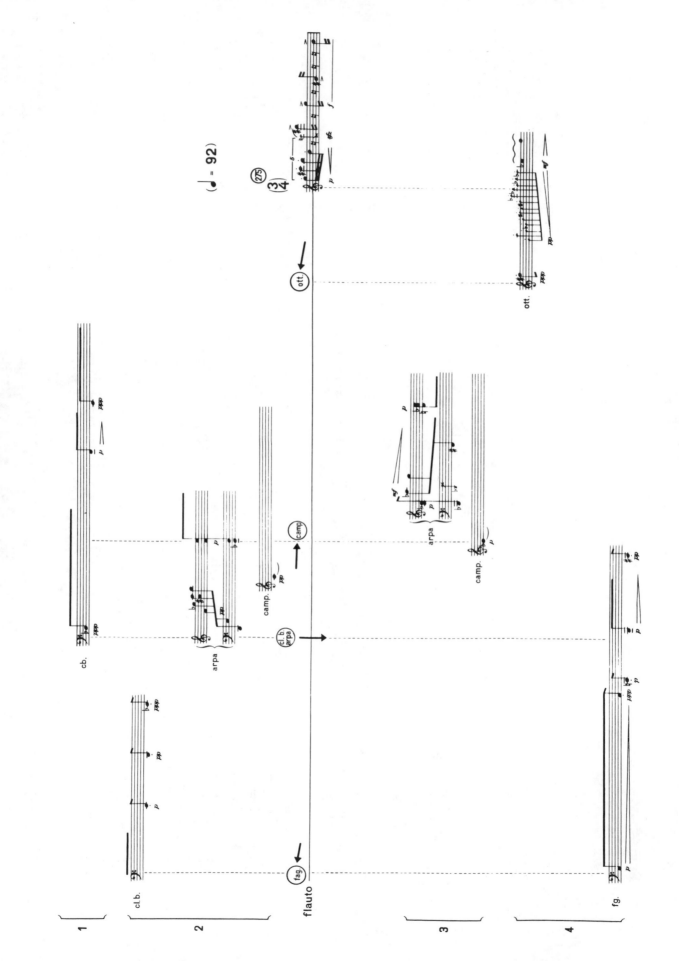

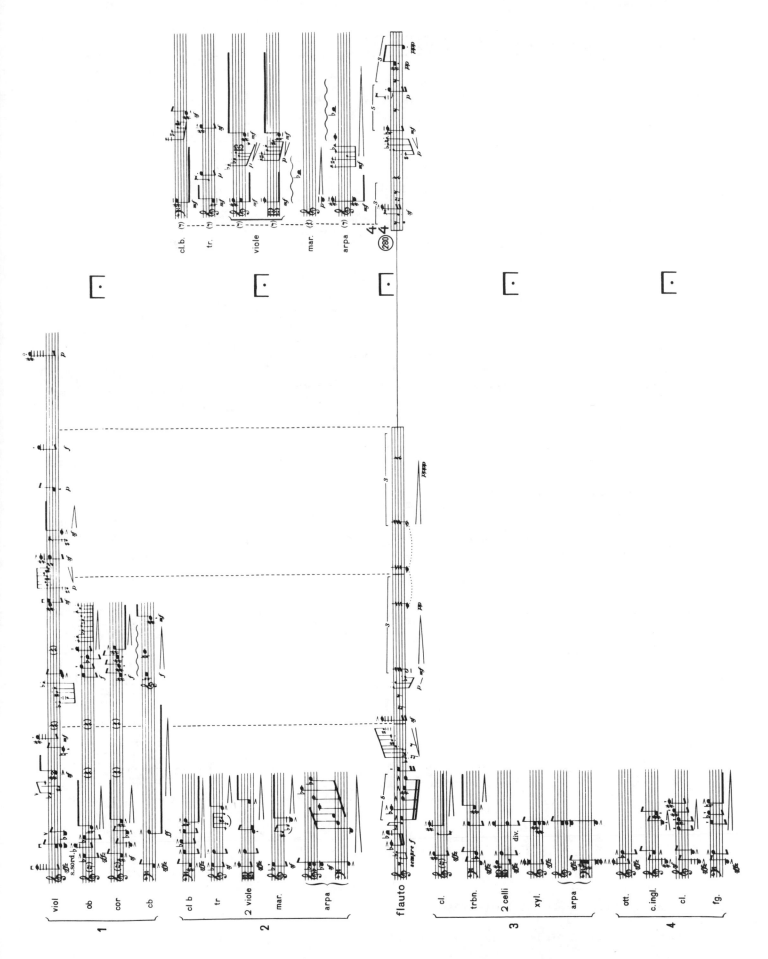

FRANZ SCHUBERT (TO A FRIEND)

DOMINICK ARGENTO

Lyrics are taken from a letter written by Schubert on 31 March 1824.

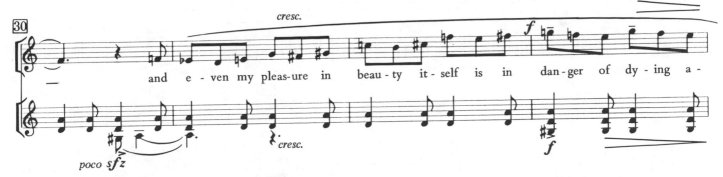

and e-ven my pleas-ure in beau-ty it-self is in dan-ger of dy-ing a-

Più mosso

way! "Mein-e Ruh' ist

hin, mein Herz ist schwer;"

Tempo I

thus sang Gretch-en at her spin - ning wheel.

So might I now sing ev-ery day, for

JOHANN SEBASTIAN BACH (TO THE TOWN COUNCIL)

DOMINICK ARGENTO

Lyrics are taken from a letter written by Bach on 24 August 17–.

mer-chant in the town of Leip - zig, was mar-ried on the twelfth of Au - gust of the pre - sent

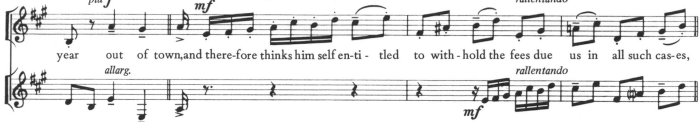

Meno mosso, gioviale

year out of town, and there-fore thinks him self en-ti - tled to with-hold the fees due us in all such cas-es,

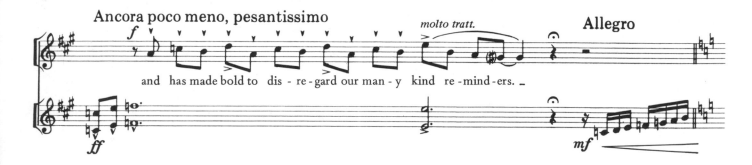

Ancora poco meno, pesantissimo   *molto tratt.*   **Allegro**

and has made bold to dis - re - gard our man - y kind re - mind - ers. _

Where - as the said fees _ make up the great - er part of our e -

mol - u - ments, a per - qui - site of this po - si - tion and

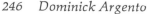

KLAVIERSTUCK VIII

KARLHEINZ STOCKHAUSEN

General Foreword

Piano Pieces V–X may be played singly, in any order desired, or mixed together with Piano Pieces I–IV.

Small notes ♭, ♫ are independent of the tempo fluctuations indicated and are played "a s f a s t a s p o s s i b l e". They are just as import-ant as large notes; they should be articulated clearly and not quasi arpeggiated. Therefore they must be executed more slowly in the lower registers than in the upper. The various intervallic leaps within groups of small notes should result in a differentiation of the actual intervals of entry (do not make them equal). Groups of small notes between vertical dotted lines ( ) i n t e r r u p t the tempo indicated.

An **accidental** (♯ ♭) applies only to the note before which it stands.

= depress right pedal all the way down.

= depress right pedal just so far down that the duration of the attack and a soft continuation of the note are audible after releasing the key. Depress pedal about halfway for notes in the middle register, one-third for the low register, two-thirds for the high register and completely for the highest register.

= left pedal is indicated at only a few places; it may, however, be used at any other place desired.

= depress the key for the duration indicated. = notes follow each other closely.

= depress key completely and gradually release, so that the note still continues but becomes more and more soft and bright. =

"portato": a short caesura between the portato note and following note.

= "staccato".

= "legato": the attack of a note and the release of the previous one sound together very briefly. Use right pedal only at leaps.

= key remains completely depressed, begin right pedal as ⌐ and gradually release. For longer durations, towards the end of the note as ⌐ without pedal.

= staccato attack with sound continuing softly.

= staccato attack immediately followed by depressing right pedal, **so that the note continues softly. The time between attack and pedal relatively long in the lower registers, minimal in the upper.**

= staccato attack immediately followed by depressing the key s i l e n t l y, so that the note continues softly after the short attack ( ). The time between the two actions is again dependent on the pitch.

= depress key silently.

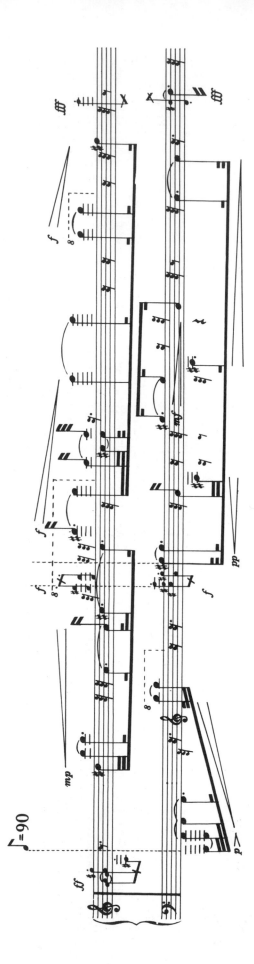

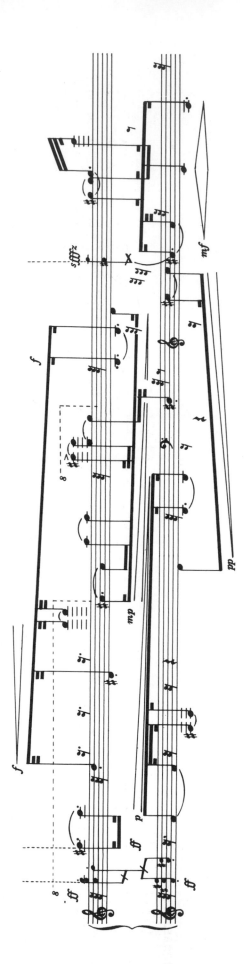

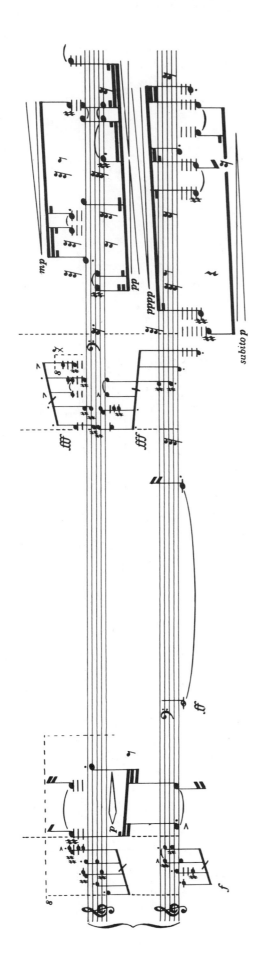
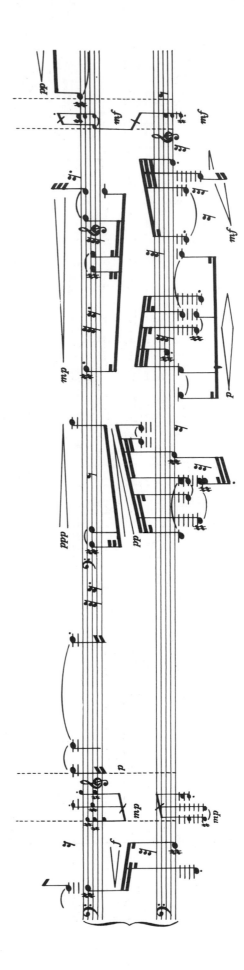

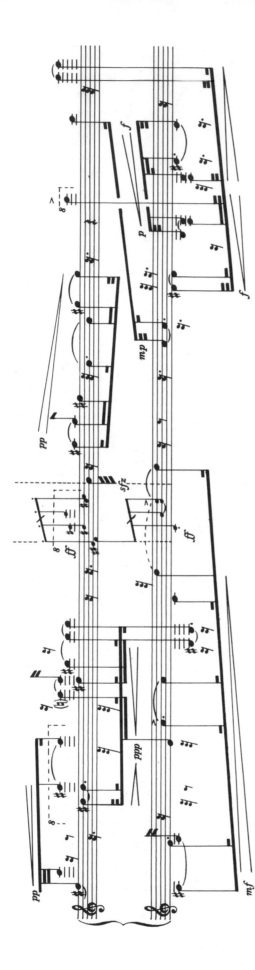
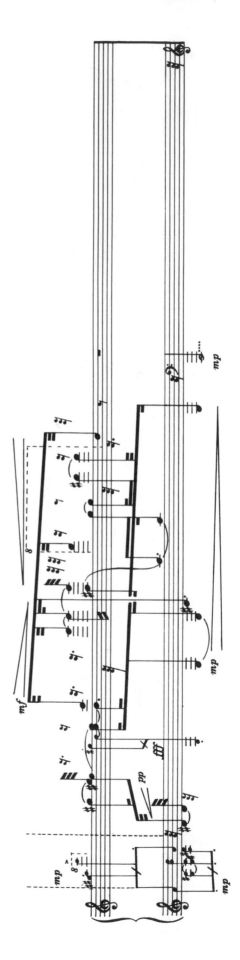

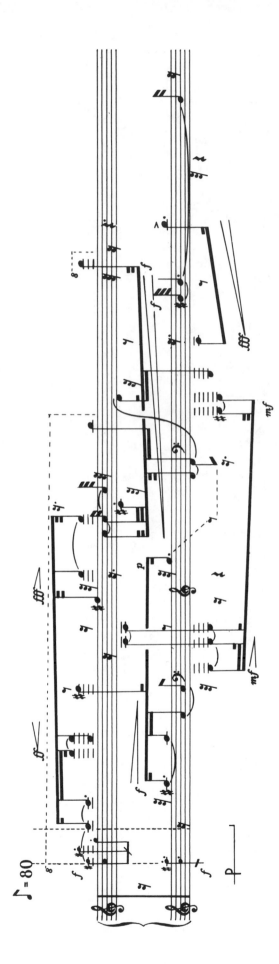
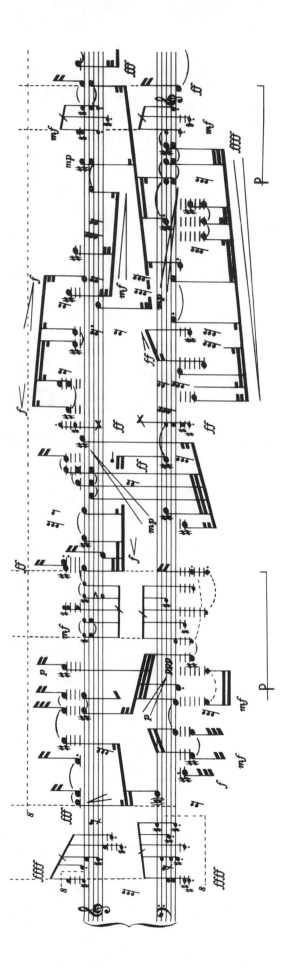

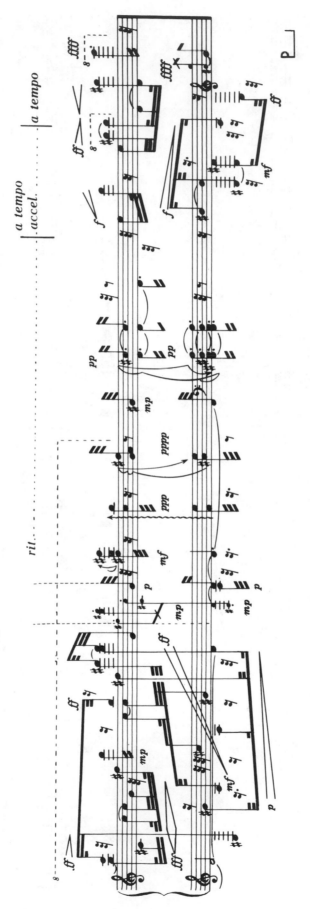

SYNCHRONISMS NO. 3 FOR CELLO AND ELECTRONIC SOUNDS

EXCERPT

MARIO DAVIDOVSKY

THE PASSION AND DEATH OF OUR LORD JESUS CHRIST ACCORDING TO ST. LUKE

PART I, EXCERPT

KRZYSTOF PENDERECKI

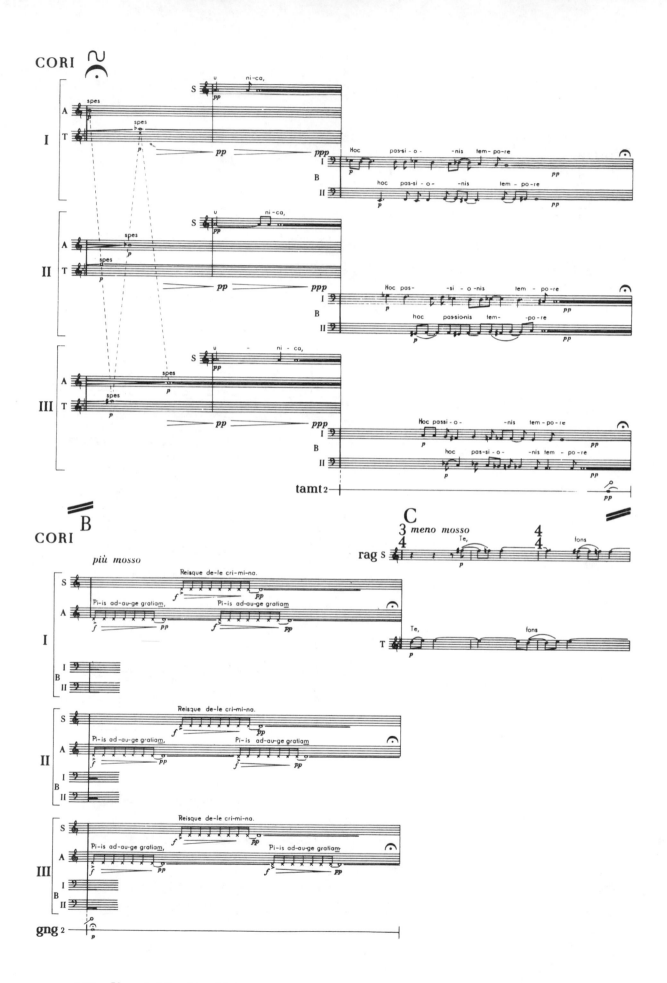

Evang: Apparuit autem illi angelus de caelo, confortans eum. Et factus in agonia, prolixius orabat. Et factus est sudor eius sicut guttae sanguinis decurrentis in terram.

* auf einem zwischen *a* und *o* liegenden Vokal singen • sing on a vowel somewhere between *a* and *o* • śpiewać na samogłosce pośredniej między *a - o*

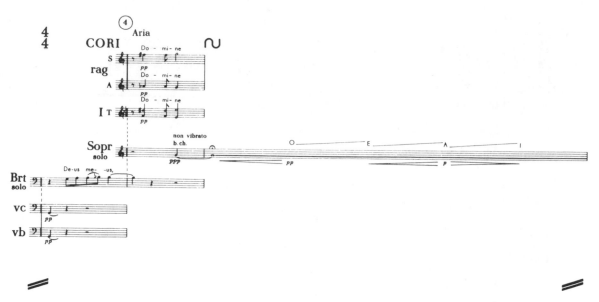

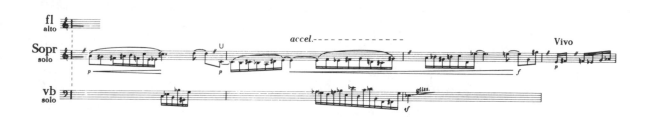

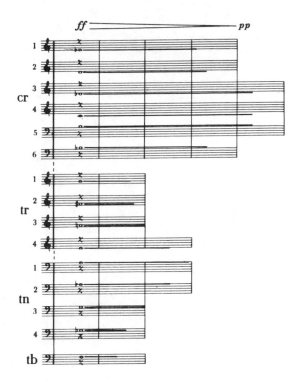

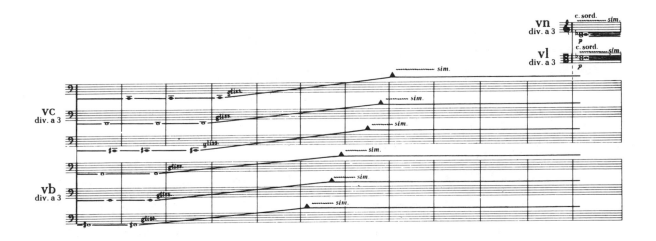

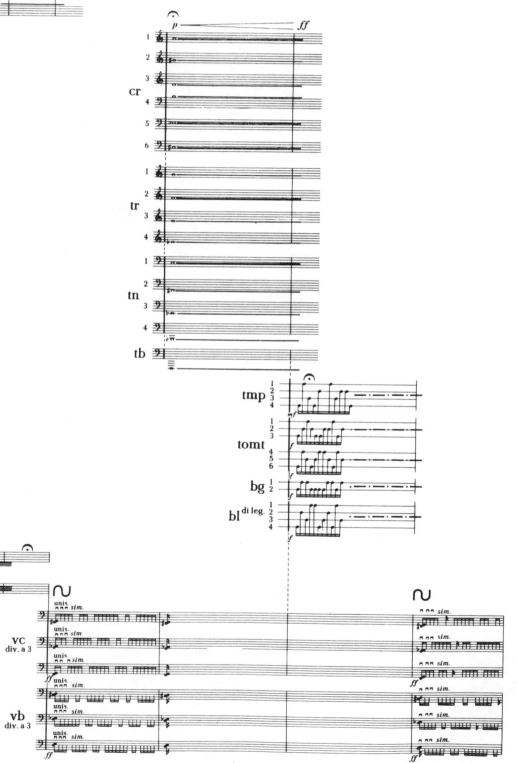

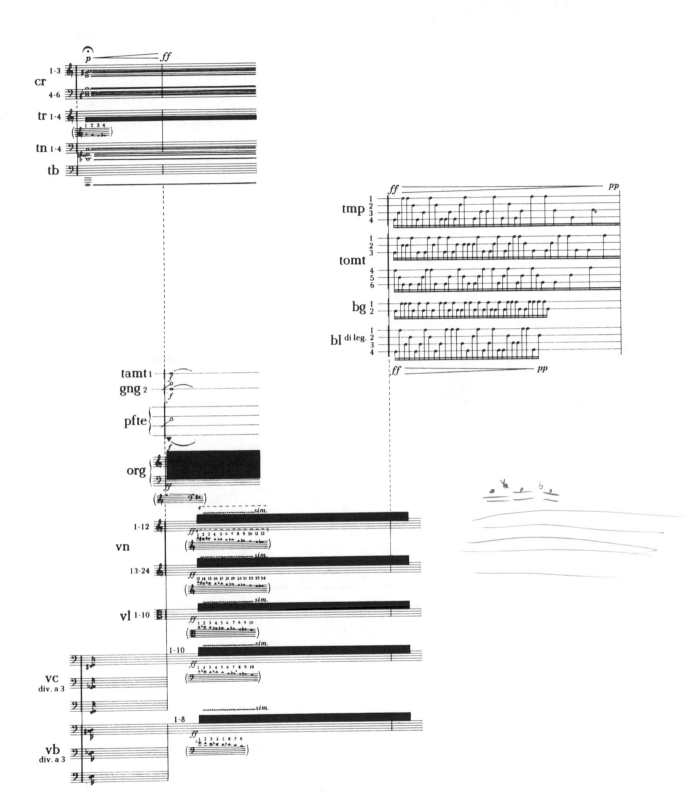

CANZONE DA SONAR FOR TENOR SAX AND PIANO

SAX KEY

THOM MASON

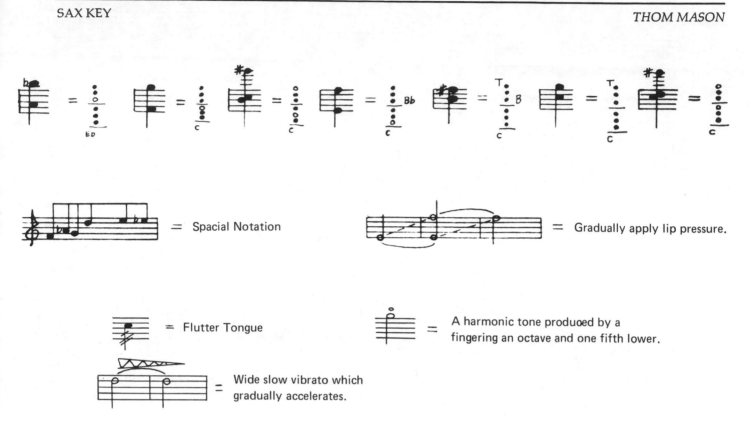

= Spacial Notation

= Gradually apply lip pressure.

= Flutter Tongue

= A harmonic tone produced by a fingering an octave and one fifth lower.

= Wide slow vibrato which gradually accelerates.

PIANO KEY

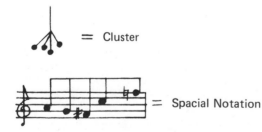

= Cluster

= Spacial Notation

= Cluster

to Fred Hemke

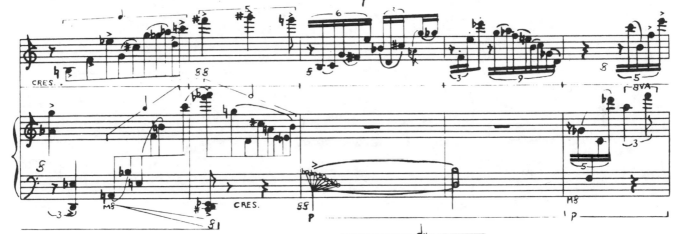

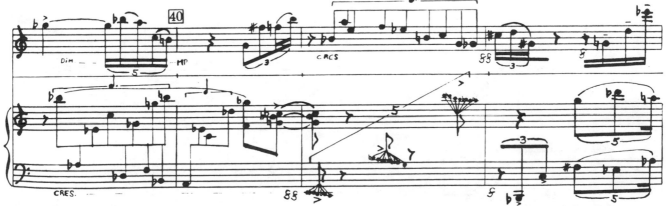

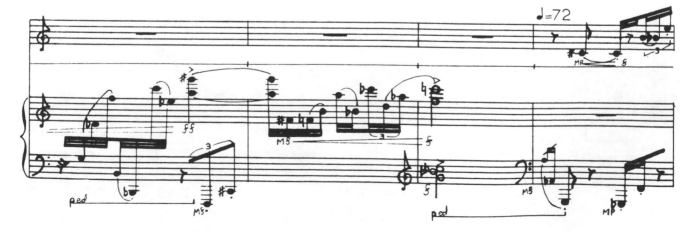

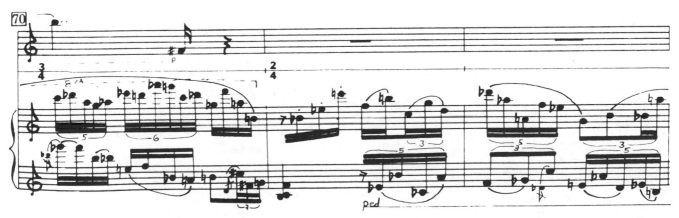

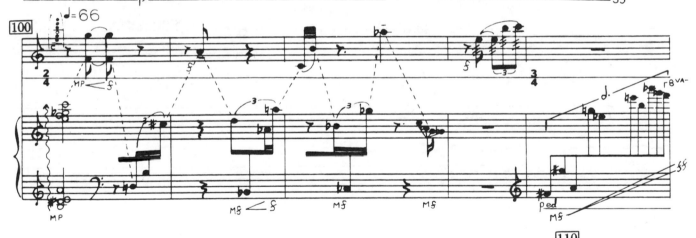

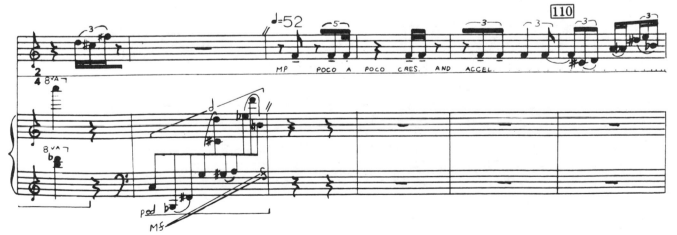

ONLY THE ORDER OF TONES IS FIXED,
NOT THE OCTAVE. PLAY IN A SLOW, UNEVEN
MANNER.

(1) Trill between natural
+ harmonic fingerings

gradually softer + slower

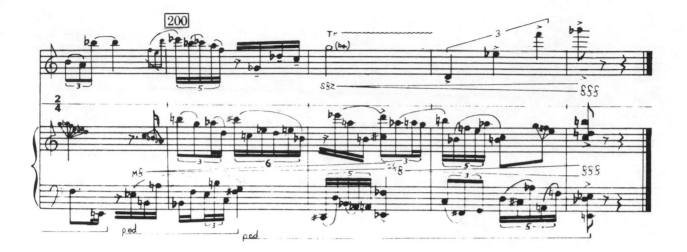

Printer and Binder: Braun-Brumfield, Inc.
80 81 82 8 7 6 5 4 3